This book attempts to present Schumann's aesthetics systematically, especially in relation to his piano music written between 1830-1840. It further essays to point out how Schumann's artistic development is closely associated with his aesthetic and critical maturation. No attempt has been made to bring forth a new theory on Schumann, but rather to clarify issues which have been misconstrued by other writers or omitted from consideration. Previously, Schumann's aesthetics have been covered cursorily in biographies and scattered articles.

To facilitate an understanding of Schumann's mind, an examination is made of the intellectual milieu in which Schumann worked. It is found that he read or was at least affected by the main stream of great romantic poets and philosophers. His prose writings mention his indebtedness to some of them, and his thinking shows the influence of others in many ways. The piano music composed between 1830-1840 reflects particularly the romantic side of his aesthetics.

Dr. Brown received his master's degree from Harvard, and his doctorate in musicology from the University of Wisconsin. Among several national fellowships, he received a grant from the German government to do research on Robert Schumann in Berlin. At present he is Professor of Music at De Paul University in Chicago.

The Aesthetics of
ROBERT SCHUMANN

The Aesthetics of
ROBERT SCHUMANN

by
THOMAS ALAN BROWN

PHILOSOPHICAL LIBRARY
New York

TO MY PARENTS

The Aesthetics of
ROBERT SCHUMANN

PREFACE

The author would like to express his gratitude to the Deutscher Akademischer Austauschdienst, which gave him a grant to do the necessary research in Germany and also to the Vilas Foundation, Madison, Wisconsin, which gave him the financial support to stay a second year in Germany and finish the project. Without the financial aid from these two organizations, he would not have been able to complete the book. He would also like to thank Professor Robert Crane of the University of Wisconsin School of Music, for his unselfish and continuous guidance. When the author was in Berlin, he received many helpful suggestions from Professor Siegfried Borris of the Berlin Hochschule für Musik and Dr. Erich-Müller von Asow, Director of the Internationales Musiker Briefarchiv. A great debt is owed to the librarians at the Free University, Berlin, and the University of Wisconsin for their aid in procuring books. Finally, the author would like to thank his parents for their continued encouragement throughout the writing of this book.

ACKNOWLEDGMENTS

The privilege of quoting musical examples from the following copyright works has been granted by the owners and is herewith gratefully acknowledged:

"24 Capricen für Violin Solo" by Paganini, Opus 1, edited by Carl Flesch, pp. 12, 26. Copyright by C. F. Peters Corp., New York; "Sonatas for Pianoforte and Violin" by Beethoven, edited by Rudolf Ganz and Leopold Auer, p. 98. Copyright MCMXVII by Carl Fischer, Inc., New York; International Copyright Secured; "The Nine Symphonies of Beethoven in Score" edited and devised by Albert E. Wier, pp. 6, 87, 88. Copyright by Harcourt, Brace & World, Inc., New York;

"Complete Works for Piano Solo" by Robert Schumann, edited by Clara Schumann; Vol. I, pp. 3, 10, 12, 13, 14, 15, 22, 23, 34, 39, 40, 45, 58, 77, 89, 105, 108, 113, 121, 125, 130, 131, 133, 169, 175; Vol. II, pp. 3, 7, 8, 15, 19, 21, 25, 53, 57, 91, 121, 127, 129; Vol. III, pp. 26, 39, 48, 53, 57, 67, 81, 83, 85, 90, 111, 112; Vol. IV, pp. 32, 45, 56, 57, 81, 111, 130, 134, 136, 137, 183; Vol. V, p. 36; Vol. VI, p. 74; published by Edwin F. Kalmus, New York, N.Y.; "Five Piano Concertos" by Beethoven (Miniature Orchestra Score), published by Edwin F. Kalmus, New York, N.Y., p. 162.

CONTENTS

CHAPTER I

INTRODUCTION

Since 1856, the year that Robert Schumann died, there has been much written about him, and various approaches to his musical and literary production have been taken. Most of these approaches, however, take the form either of biography or stylistic analysis,[1] while little has been written on Schumann's aesthetics. It is our purpose in this book to attempt to integrate Schumann's ideas on aesthetics into a coherent system, with special attention given to the reflection of these concepts in his piano music. Although Schumann made several starts at writing a treatise on aesthetics, he never completed one. Consequently, most of his ideas on the subject appear in a few fragments, for example *Ästhetische Fragmente und Aphorismen zur Ästhetik der Musik, Die Tonwelt, Aus dem Tagebuch der Hl. Cecilia*, and *Juniusabende und Julitage;* and also in letters and reviews for the *Neue Zeitschrift für Musik*, a musical journal he and his friends founded.

Before examining Schumann's thought, we will present first those romantic ideas which influenced Schumann. Although Schumann read widely, and was affected by many writers, only those who had the greatest impact on Schumann's thought have been selected, for example, Jean Paul, Wackenroder, Tieck, Thibaut, E. T. A. Hoffmann, Hegel, and Schopenhauer. Other important figures in the intellectual climate of the time such as Lessing and the Encyclopedists, while certainly known to Schumann, will not be discussed because their direct influence on him is not significant.

In the next section of this book we will investigate Schumann's aesthetic principles. Most of his ideas on music, it will be seen, are derived from these principles. Furthermore, we will endeavor to show the connection between Schumann's general aesthetics and his ideas both on music as an art form and on the composition of piano music. Also, as will be shown, the criteria which Schumann established for evaluating the work of a critic are based on these principles.

These two chapters of background material are of particular importance for understanding Schumann's conception of music, a matter which is discussed in two later chapters. His conception is derived from a curious blending of classicism and romanticism, restraint and freedom, study and inspiration, literature and music. Basically Schumann was a creator, and his aesthetic principles are primarily an outgrowth of his artistic endeavors. Although Schumann derived most of his ideas on music from these principles, he also could compose without any regard for abstract thought. It also was possible for Schumann to formulate aesthetic principles on the basis of previously conceived compositions. His life perpetually moved between the world of music and that of philosophy, without ever allying itself permanently with either. This is similar to movement in Hegelian dialectic. As Hegel states,

By reason of the nature of the method which has been demonstrated the science is seen to be a circle which returns upon itself, for mediation bends back its end into its beginning or simple ground. Further, this circle is a circle of circles; for each member, being inspired by the method, is intro-Reflection which, returning to the beginning, is at the same time the beginning of a new member.[2]

Similarly Schumann's personality was composed of two conflicting sides, the passionate and the dreamy, which were represented in the characters of Florestan and Eusebius and which seldom were satisfactorily reconciled.

Finally, we will attempt to define Schumann's meaning of the term "programmatic music", and then illustrate it through examples from his piano compositions.

One of the most common criticisms leveled against Schumann is that he was not a philosopher.[3] In the strict sense of the term he was not, but he was deeply interested in those philosophic concepts which provided the aesthetic basis for his music. In fact, there is a surprising parallel between Schumann's career and the movement of philosophic and artistic concepts from about 1775 to 1870. During these years, art and philosophy move from the classicism and rationalism of the eighteenth century to romanticism and idealism and finally back again to the restraint of the Victorian era. Schumann, although basically a romantic, follows this pattern in miniature. Before 1830, he is influenced by classic ideas on art; during the 1830's by romantic concepts; and sometime after 1840 to his death he reverts to more and more classic principles.

The years of Schumann's most romantic period, from about 1830-1840, will be the focal point of this book. Moreover, because of limitations of space, only his piano music will be discussed in detail; the songs of 1840, typically romantic, might well form the basis of a similar book on the relation of Schumann's aesthetics to his composition of *Lieder*.

The romantic era and Schumann's romantic period both reached a high point during the 1830s. Before 1830 Schumann followed the forms of his more classic predecessors. The Polonaise, the quartet, and unwritten improvisations (similar to Beethoven's) characterized his early period. Another example of his early classicism is his youthful and unfinished Symphony in G Minor, which follows the classical model of a symphony, and exhibits the influence of Beethoven.[4] Gradually these forms were replaced by the romantic pieces of Schumann's middle period. And so the early Polonaises were adapted for use in *Papillons*, and improvised portraits of his friends were changed to written characterizations, as in *Carnaval*.

After 1840, in his treatment of piano music, Schumann reacted against the unbounded enthusiasm of romanticism and returned to more classical forms. In this period he wrote six studies which employed canonic devices (Opus 56), fugues (Opus 72), a piano concerto, and chamber music with piano. In vocal music, the song is replaced by the opera and oratorios. His approach toward childhood changes from the romantic *Kinderszenen* to the more classic *Album für die Jugend*, Opus 68, which employs such baroque forms as chorale, sicilian, canon and fugue.

This pattern in music follows the classic-romantic-classic cycle. At the end of the eighteenth century and the beginning of the nineteenth the great classicists were at the height of their creative powers. Then the romantics reached their zenith during the 1830s. Finally, there is a return toward a new classicism. As Jacques Barzun writes in his book on Berlioz, "After 1840 one discerns . . . a movement steadily diverging from the main evolution of Romanticism and its various offshoots. This once again calls itself Classicism."[5]

Berlioz underwent a somewhat similar transition, although one could not go so far as to call him a classicist. In his early years he admired the work of such classic composers as Gluck and Beethoven; but he was clearly romantic in his own work. The *Symphonie Fantastique*, written when Berlioz was twenty-six, is one of the first revolutionary works in the romantic style. Then

9

in his later years works such as *L'Enfance du Christ* manifest the restraint of a more classic style. As Elliot writes, ". . . he began as an ardent romantic and ended, if not precisely as a classic, at least as one who leaned more and more towards the classical ideal of line as opposed to colour." [6]

On a larger scale, one can see a parallel in the other arts and in philosophy. English literature moves from the measured couplets of Pope to the freedom of Wordsworth back to the discipline of Tennyson. In German literature, Heinrich Heine displays a similar change, from early classical influences to the romanticism of the *Buch der Lieder* (published in 1827), back to the classicism of his satires of the 1840s.

Philosophy moves from the rationalism of Leibniz and Locke to the idealism of Kant and Hegel and finally to the pessimism of Schopenhauer, the positivism of Comte, and the atheism of Nietzsche. The parallel in philosophy, however, is not so much a return to the rationalism of the seventeenth and eighteenth centuries as it is a reaction to the falsely optimistic aspects of idealism.

With all these factors in mind, we will endeavor to present an exposition of Schumann's ideas, as an aid for the greater understanding of his life, his writings, and his compositions.

CHAPTER II

THE ROMANTIC MILIEU OF ROBERT SCHUMANN

A consideration of the aesthetics of Robert Schumann requires an understanding of his intellectual milieu. One cannot examine the ideas of a great genius *in vacuo*.

The most important intellectual force affecting Schumann was the romantic movement. It is frequently stated that in the late eighteenth and early nineteenth century there was a change in the current of thought. This new attitude toward man and his increased preeminence in the great chain of being was reflected in the aesthetics of the romantics.

Aesthetics meant a turn to individuality, to the concrete response of the individual: it prepared the way to a true understanding of history, not as something dead and schematic, but as a living process.[7]

This turn to individuality also occurred in the renaissance when a similar shift in the micro-macrocosm relationship took place.[8] However, the change in the early nineteenth century should not be regarded as a sudden and complete break with the past; rather, it should be viewed as a gradual evolution, conserving some of the old in the midst of the new. Remnants of eighteenth century thought were part of the fabric of nineteenth century ideas, just as germs of romantic thought existed in the preceding classical age. Therefore, the enhanced importance of man should be interpreted as a development in emphasis rather than a complete reversal of beliefs and ideals.

In order to understand the relationship of romantic aesthetics to Schumann's thought one must investigate the ideas of representative men who influenced his thinking. In many instances one knows exactly which writers Schumann read and a direct connection can be drawn, but one also must realize what ideas were *en vogue*, since these too undoubtedly had an influence on his thinking. First, the earlier romantic aestheticians who left a direct imprint on Schumann will be considered and next the idealistic philosophers, Hegel and Schopenhauer, whose ideas were current during the first half of the nineteenth century.

11

The ideas of Johann Gottfried von Herder (1744-1803), an eighteenth century pre-romantic, are important in understanding romanticism. No attempt will be made to discuss systematically his aesthetics of music, but rather only to show how he foreshadows the romantics and how the germs of some of his ideas are later enlarged upon by nineteenth century thinkers. Since it is usually common for initiators of new movements to search for links with the past, it was natural for the romantics to turn to Herder for inspiration. Herder's principles of criticism contain the notion of an aristocracy of talent. He believes that only the genius is capable of criticizing the works of another genius. ". . . criticism without genius is nothing. Only a genius can judge and teach another." [9]

Throughout the nineteenth century a controversy arose questioning the superiority of music over poetry. This theme was anticipated by Herder.

Music without words places us in a region of obscure ideas; it awakens emotions, for each in his own way; emotions as they lie dormant in the heart, which, lacking words, find no guidepost and leader in the stream, or in the flood, of artistic tones. . . . Through . . . music the soul can be placed outside itself in such a manner that, rendered useless and indifferent to this earthly life, it loses itself in formless . . . tones.[10]

Herder shows a similarity to later aestheticians in his conception of the relationship between music and nature. From nature the artist derives the model and inspiration for his art, and indirectly from the One, i.e., God, the creator of nature. In the romantic age, union with the One was thought to be helped by a close communion with nature.

Everything, therefore, which resounds in nature is music; it has its elements in itself, and requires only a hand to lure it forth, an ear to hear it, a sympathy to perceive it. No artist invented any tone or gave it any power which it did not already possess in nature and in his instrument; he discovered it, however, and forced it forward with sweet power.[11]

Of the romantic writers who followed Herder in time and to a certain extent in thought, Johann Paul Richter (1763-1825) is particularly significant for Schumann. Schumann regards him, along with Bach, as his guide and artistic father.[12] Jean Paul's theories on aesthetics may be found in his novels, especially *Flegeljahre,* but his most comprehensive work on this subject is his book *Die Vorschule der Ästhetik*. In this book he discusses his views on art with special reference to music.

One of the major problems which confronted the romantics was the function of art. Not only was stress laid on the role of the artist in society, but also on what should be demanded from art. Jean Paul sees art as a totality, with every participating element having its peculiar function. A masterpiece should not be only an exercise of artistic talent but in addition an attempt to understand the more subtle and enigmatic aspects of the world. He shuns the classical view of art in favor of a conception which emphasizes its directing nature.

Jean Paul wishes to avoid two extremes, the particular which slavishly copies nature, and the general which disregards the world entirely. "Art should be the union of the particular and the general. It does not copy and it must not annihilate the world. Rather it should decipher its mysterious language. Thus poetry cannot be teaching. It offers signs." [13]

For Jean Paul, art has a metaphysical function. Anticipating Schopenhauer, he believes that music does not conjure up single events or feelings, but rather a universal and mystic yearning to unite with the One. Music is the link between man and the angels and a means by which man may overcome his loneliness.

. . . music is the echo from a transcendent harmonious world; it is the sigh of the angel within us. When the word is silent . . . and when our mute hearts lie lonely behind the ribcage of our chest, then it is only through music that men call to each other in their dungeons, and unite their distant sighs in their wilderness.[14]

Music not only has the function of uniting men metaphysically with the angels, but also of uniting the past with the future. For Jean Paul it imparts a mysterious vision of the past and future which cannot clearly be distinguished in the intellect, but touches the heart with a mood at once reflective and anticipative. As he writes in *Flegeljahre*, "Divine music shows man a past and a future which he never otherwise experiences." [15] And in *Hesperus* there is a similar passage which reads "O music, you that bring the past and the future with its flying flames so close to our wounds, are you the evening breeze from this life or the morning air from yonder?" [16] Jean Paul poignantly describes the power of music.

How many hours and souls and bodies must be arrayed one after the other in order to bring about only a single inner exaltation [*Innen-*

13

feier], which you receive from music in one minute as if from invisible hands? I have wept greatly and blessedly, as much as you can imagine: music repeats the feelings in your heart and brings back to you all the tears.[17]

Jean Paul's discussion and definition of genius in his book on aesthetics apparently had a great influence on Schumann.[18] Jean Paul is not concerned with describing the function of the genius in society, but rather in attempting to define him. In his analysis he first enumerates the characteristics which distinguish the genius from ordinary man, and then classifies the different stages of genius. He states that the genius differs from other people quantitatively. The genius has the vision necessary to peer into nature and discover its secrets.

The genius differs, in so far as he sees nature more richly and more completely, as man differs from the half-blind and half-deaf animals. . . . The true poet, in his wedding of art to nature, will imitate the park-gardener, who knows how to weave his garden into the surroundings of nature as if they were boundless continuities, but on a higher level he will surround confined nature with the limitlessness of the Idea and let the former disappear in the latter as if ascending to heaven.[19]

Also, Jean Paul believes that the artist perpetually strives to shape the formless elements of nature and coalesce them into a work of art. He strives to fathom the complexities not only of this world but also of the next. One of the greatest differences between the ordinary man and the artistic genius is that the artist teaches the world, rather than the world the artist. In the end he strives to unite nature and the mind of man in a harmonious whole.

If, however, there are men in whom the divine instinct speaks more clearly and distinctly than in others;—if he teaches one of them to perceive the terrestrial (rather than the terrestrial teaching him);—if he gives and knows a viewpoint of the whole: then harmony and beauty from both worlds will be reflected and united, since in the eyes of the gods there is only oneness and no contradiction of parts. And that is genius; and the reconciliation of both worlds is the so-called Ideal.[20]

Although Jean Paul describes genius in these rather abstract terms, he is more concrete when he enumerates the two qualities which are inherent in every genius. The first of these is instinct. The genius is able to penetrate matters and extract their quintessence, as opposed to the imitator who is content to recognize material in its outer form. Combined with instinct, the genius

14

possesses economy and the power to contemplate. "How does divine sensibility distinguish itself from the sinful?—Through the instinct of the unconsciousness and the love for it." [21] Many authors discuss the necessity for imagination. Jean Paul does not omit this element from the list of qualities ascribed to genius; he takes it for granted and considers it a necessity for both the genius and the talented.

The power of imagination is the prose of creative power [*Bildungkraft*] or fantasy. It is nothing but a highly intensified, brightly colored memory which animals also possess, since they dream and fear. . . . But fantasy or creative power is something higher; it is the World-Soul of all souls and the elementary spirit of the remaining powers.[22]

Two of the three stages of creativity described by Jean Paul influenced Schumann. The first includes those who have talent and are endowed with fantasy, which enables them to view matters partially. The talented man has a sharp mind, wit, understanding, and mathematical and historical perspective. In contrast to the genius, the talented has the gift of being able to comprehend phases of life, but never all of it. "That of the talented is only partial; it is not that high degree of separation of the inner world from itself, but only approximately from the outer world." [23] The talented man can rise above the world about him and thus achieve a measure of the poetic vision; but he does not reach the sublimity of the true poet, who can rise above himself and unite with the Creative Spirit.

The highest level of creativity is found in the genius, whose qualities have been enumerated. The genius, in the eyes of Jean Paul is the most valuable member of society. He relies on the unconscious, which is the outstanding gift of a poet. "The most powerful force within the poet, that which endows his work with the good and the evil soul, is precisely the unconscious." [24]

In the writings of Jean Paul there are many ideas which influence Schumann's thoughts about the relationship between poetry and music. Both men are concerned with determining which art form can express man's emotions more adequately. They agree that music is better suited for this function, although they also believe that both poetry and music are inextricably bound together.

The following story from *Aussprache des Herzens*, by Jean Paul, is indicative of this attitude.

Once upon a time the loving Genius of those blessed with richer emotions appeared before Jupiter and begged: "Divine Father, give

15

thy people a better language, for they have only words, when they want to say how they grieve, how they rejoice, how they love." "Did I not give them the tear," said Jupiter, "The tear of joy, and the tear of sorrow and the sweeter one of love." The Genius replied: "Even the tear is not sufficient to express what is in the heart. Divine Father, give them a better language whenever they wish to say how they feel infinite yearning, how the morning star of childhood follows them, and the rose-aurora of youth glows and how before them in old age, the golden evening clouds of a future life glow and hover high above the lost sun. My Father, give them a new language for the heart!" Now Jupiter, through the music of the spheres heard the muse of song approach, and he beckoned to her and said: "Descend to mankind and teach them your language." Then the muse of song came down to us and taught [us] tones; and since then the human heart can speak.[25]

Another influence on Schumann was *Phantasien über die Kunst,* which was the joint effort of Wilhelm Heinrich Wackenroder (1773-1798) and Ludwig Tieck (1773-1853). Throughout history there have been controversies about the relative value of the arts. For example, in the renaissance the *Dialogues* of Francisco D'Ollanda debate the merits of painting over sculpture and architecture. Michelangelo is presented defending the superiority of painting.[26] In the romantic era, the debate revolved around the value of music as opposed to poetry. The romantics were more concerned with the effect art had on its public, i.e., its ability to arouse dormant emotions and sensations. In the following quotation Wackenroder and Tieck conclude that music is more powerful than words, an idea which was to be expanded upon later by Schopenhauer.

Language counts, names, and describes its metamorphoses in alien material; music pours it forth to us herself. . . . In the mirror of tones the human soul learns to know itself; it is through them that we learn to feel emotion; they give living consciousness to many a dreamy spirit in the obscure corners of the soul and enrich our inner being with completely new magical spirits of emotion.[27]

Since music possesses this overwhelming emotional power, it is logical to conclude that it can evoke moods and sensations. Wackenroder and Tieck put great importance on the magical state of ecstasy which music creates. The listener attains a state of semi-consciousness in which he is not sure of Time or Being.

I consider music the most wonderful of these inventions, because it portrays human emotions in a super-human way, because it shows above our heads all movements of our souls incorporeally, clothed in golden clouds of airy harmonies, because it speaks a language which

16

we do not know in daily life, a language we have learned, we know not where?—nor how?—and which one only should like to consider as the language of the angels.[28]

Music is the medium for the transmission of this alien tongue. Wackenroder and Tieck revere art and warn against overemphasizing the artist's role. "Truly, it is art which one must respect, not the artist; he is nothing more than a weak tool!"[29] However, they recognize that a select group of talented individuals may be drawn together by mutual understanding. Thus, an artist is only understood by a select group. "An artist ought to be an artist just for himself, for his own heart's delight and for one or two people who understand him."[30] Wackenroder and Tieck also discuss the problem of the dichotomy between rules and inspiration. They admit the necessity for rules although they maintain that if the artist composes only according to a set pattern, he is not creating but merely writing exercises. Wackenroder, writing about a fictitious musician named Joseph Berglinger, expresses his own view of art behind this mask.

Joseph Berglinger, the musician who had felt its inspiration like a divine intoxication (the more potent the darker and more mysterious its language), is indignant when he discovers that art is craft, that all melodies are based on a single mathematical law, that "instead of flying freely" he "had to climb around in the clumsy scaffolding and cage of the grammar of art" and learn its laborious mechanics.[31]

One of the most influential books on the aesthetics of music in the early nineteenth century, and a work which Schumann often praised, is Friedrich Thibaut's (1774-1840) *Ueber Reinheit der Tonkunst*, which first appeared in 1825. Thibaut attempts to elucidate three main points. First of all he desires a revival of renaissance and baroque music, which was not readily accessible to contemporary composers.

Thus our so-called virtuosi, music directors and teachers carefully circumvent the old and try to debase in every way endless musical treasures of which we can be so proud; one can get away with it quite easily.[32]

Thibaut contends that only through a knowledge of earlier music can an appreciation of the contemporary be obtained.

It has never been recognized so completely as today that an historical study and knowledge of existent classics is and should be the basis for all genuine scholarship. Steady progress can be made only if one is taught through the teaching of others and seeks to promote the worthwhile with zeal.[33]

17

Thibaut criticizes severely those who are only concerned with contemporary music and who do not essay to learn the literature of preceding centuries.

Everywhere it is considered necessary, not only to live in the present, but also to enjoy the works of all times, because it is very easy to learn thereby and because, as a rule every period also has its own special virtue.[34]

The second reason for writing his book is implicit in the title, *On the Purity of Music*. With this title he implies its ethical purity. To him music is something apart from and higher than worldly matters, and superior to other arts. That is, through music one may be purified; and Thibaut regrets the present dearth of musicians, especially in the church, who would serve its true function.

Music should represent all states of sensation, of emotion and of passion but poetically, and not, therefore, as they exist in a degenerated form, but as they really stand in strength and purity.[35]

". . . that is just the limitlessness of perfect music, that it can stimulate, purify, and ennoble the soul and heart in all respects." [36] His aforementioned plea for a revival of older music is also motivated by the fact that masters of previous generations had fulfilled this religious obligation.

Thibaut's work reveals a desire to see man not only as cleansed through music, but also as possessing a broad range of musical taste. For Thibaut, everything has its appropriate place in the universe and should be appreciated for its own worth. In his view, it is meaningless to make such comparisons as that between the value of instrumental and vocal music.

I do not deny the specific charm of instruments, . . . the graceful, the fleeting, the leaping, the swirling, the impetuous and rhythmical gaiety can be imitated much better, a thousand times better, if you please, with instruments than with voices. However, everything stands in its place, where it belongs.[37]

To Thibaut the place of the artist in the world, and specifically the genius, is significant. The genius brings imagination and a new dimension to music which others are incapable of accomplishing. He possesses a license to disregard rules which often bind the talented. This is not to imply that he is given complete freedom to break them at will, but through his insight he is able to circumvent many laws which bind others.

. . . the genius despises stringent rules as little as [he despises] hard

18

work, and only vain stupidity strives for ruleless ease, because to it is given neither the power of due obedience nor the correct ability to rule.[38]

Throughout the early romantic years a distinction between the talented man and the genius was made. The genius, according to Thibaut, creates only by adding the inexplicable extra ingredient. An artist who works only according to rules, without bringing anything novel to his work, is not an artist, but rather a talented student. The genuine creator is able to produce works which rise above ordinary assigned exercises. "A composition which does not offer anything to the emotion or which injures the sensibilities is and remains nothing more than, at the most, an exercise." [39]

E. T. A. Hoffmann (1776-1822) differs somewhat from Thibaut in his approach to the problem of the artist. Hoffmann emphasizes the artist who is misunderstood by the world. He attacks the tasteless Philistines who, when they display any interest in art, exhibit it as an ornament, rather than experiencing it as an integral part of their lives. Their taste is old-fashioned; they are opposed to any modern trends.

Hoffmann is of the opinion that music, through tone-painting, has the power to portray emotional experiences of the world. ". . . but the fact should not be overlooked that instrumental music possesses a certain means to draw into its domain occurrences of the outside world." [40]

To Hoffmann music possesses a unique characteristic. It is a secret language which is capable of appealing to man's innermost feelings and awakens in him an emotionally charged existence.

Is not music the mysterious language of a more distant spiritual realm whose wonderful accents strike a responsive chord within us, and awaken a higher and more intensive life? All passions, armed glitteringly and splendidly, fight with each other and dissolve in an unutterable yearning which fills our breast.[41]

Hoffmann believes that music is above the mundane:

It unlocks for man an unknown realm, a world which has nothing in common with outward [sensible] existence, a world in which he renounces every distinct feeling in order to commit himself wholly to an inexpressible yearning. All tone-painting which violates this inborn essence of music is to be rejected.[42]

In addition to the early romantic aestheticians, the nineteenth century idealistic philosophers, such as Georg Wilhelm Friedrich Hegel (1770-1831) and Arthur Schopenhauer (1788-1860), also influenced Schumann. Emphasis will be placed on those concepts which will be shown to be extant in Schumann's thought. There is no evidence that Schumann systematically read Hegel and Schopenhauer and no proof can be exhibited to show their influence. But these ideas were alive for the greater part of Schumann's life, and they can be seen reflected in his own writing.

Hegel's notion of art is a logical development of the Hegelian Ideal. Hegel believes that the basic reality in the world is the spirit. The spirit or God is revealed slowly in time and space as history moves on. And so in art the basic reality is beauty, an Ideal or spiritual reality which reveals itself gradually to man. Man does not really create beauty but rather he is the instrument of the world spirit underlying all matter. And so art is intuitive and emotional. It springs perforce from the poet. Creation is not an art of intellect and will, but of emotion and intuition.

One of Hegel's most important concepts is a view of art as the blending of the general with the particular. This view reflects the thinking of the earlier romantic aestheticians, but with Hegel beauty becomes an Ideal, which is made concrete as it becomes a work of art. Hegel believes that art "makes the sensuous spiritual and spiritual sensuous." [43]

Another important theme in Hegel's aesthetics is the role emotion plays in art. Music, or art in general, is an idealization of emotions. One cannot describe accurately the impressions derived from a musical composition:

They are not actual emotions which the composer puts into his works, but rather ideal illusionary feelings [*Scheingefühle*], which, disassociated from his real self, live only in his fantasy, and which further react only on the fantasy of the listener, so that the latter's real feelings also are excluded.[44]

For Hegel this *Idee der Innerlichkeit* is brought to reality in music. Hegel uses the expression *Idee der Innerlichkeit* to mean that Idea which works in the soul of man to produce art. While akin to fantasy, it is rather the ineluctable working of the spirit in man. Sound is the realization of this inwardness which enables music to become the art of emotions. "Art has the power and the mission to represent, through the means of sense perception, the idea absolute, conscious and free from all dross." [45] Hegel discovers in music the most profound manifestation of intuition, since music is capable of grasping and conveying the more subjective experiences, and thereby exciting man's emotions.

For it is precisely this sphere, the inner faculty, the abstract self-perception, which music encompasses and thereby motivates inner

20

changes within the heart and soul, as the simple concentrated center of the entire man.[46]

It is important to examine Hegel's ideas in relation to programmatic music, because these concepts are reflected in Schumann's thought. With these idealistic conceptions as a basis, Hegel discusses the ability of music to conjure up programmatic associations. He does not deny its power to awaken in man certain pictures or evoke associations, but claims that these pictures are not inherent in the music. Music can only represent indefinite emotions and moods, but man brings to a composition reminiscences which are activated by music.

A musical composition can, under certain conditions, awaken in us definite ideas and mental images. However, this is our mental image and idea, evoked to be sure by the musical composition, but not immediately by itself in terms of its musical treatment.[47]

Hegel makes a distinction between the ability of poetry, as opposed to music, to convey emotions. Music only represents in an approximate fashion the inner complexities of an emotion, while poetry represents ideas, emotions, and views exactly. According to Hegel, poetry operates in a self-confined world, while music overrides the boundaries of any circumscribed area, and consequently its sphere of action is increased.

All the nuances of gaiety, joyousness, joviality, capriciousness, praise and jubilation of the soul find their way into music, as well as the gradations of fear, worry, sadness, lamentation, sorrow, pain, yearning, reverence, admiration and love. But music does not express them with the same exactness as does poetry. Music can only approach an ever more indefinite sympathy with the movements of emotion, whereas poetry moulds views, emotions, and thoughts of a self-enclosed world of events, stories, humors, and outbursts of passion, and in this way produces works in which all of reality, reality in terms of outward appearance as well as in terms of inner substance, becomes a view and idea for our spiritual sensation. It lies in the nature of music that it can and should throw into relief a less exact and special essence in a more universal way than other arts.[48]

In Hegel one has an eloquent statement of the idealization of music. In the eighteenth century the emphasis was more on *l'art pour l'art*, and a consequent concern with the problems of form above content. With the nineteenth century and its enhancing of man's position in the great chain of being, more attention was paid to the inner meaning of music. The empirical and objective questions stood in the shadow of the subjective.

It is in this atmosphere that one must understand Hegel's posi-

21

tion. Ideas which had been expressed loosely and unsystematically by Wackenroder and Tieck, Jean Paul and Hoffmann, are more fully systematized by Hegel.

Hegel recognizes music as an Ideal, and his intention is to approach it through a dialectic search. This was reflected in the contemporary ethic which valued the striving for virtue more than virtue itself. This is an evolutionary ethic, an ethic which is more than a regulation of existing circumstances.

Music must possess in its realm of tone expedients which are capable of portraying the struggle of opposites. It is given such means in the dissonant chords. The more profound music should not only, in its course, approach the border of absolute consonance, . . . but on the contrary, the first simple combination must be torn apart into dissonances. Only in those contrasts are the deeper relationships and secrets of harmony established, and thus the deeply penetrating movements of melody can find their foundation only in the deeper relationships and secrets of harmony.[49]

The concept of music as being evolutionary is altered somewhat in Schopenhauer's philosophy. Art "repeats the eternal Ideas grasped through pure contemplation, the essential and abiding in all phenomena of the world."[50] As did Hegel, Schopenhauer holds that these Ideas are not Ideas in the Platonic sense but a concrete universal unfolded to man in the work of art.

The Idea, he emphasizes over and over again, is intuitive and not conceptual: although representing an infinite number of particular things, it is nevertheless thoroughly determined. It is never known by an individual as such, but only by one who has risen above all willing and individuality to become a pure subject of knowing.[51]

Schopenhauer, more than any of his predecessors, aims at clarifying the Ideal content of music in all its depth, by recognizing the Idea as the essential matter which an art work evokes. In his basic conception of the function of music, he is close to Hegel, since they both view music as a means of expressing indefinite emotions, moods, and sensations.

It does not express . . . this or that single, exact joy, this or that affliction, or pain, or fright, or jubilation, or happiness, or calmness, but rather joy, affliction, pain, fright, jubilation, happiness, calmness itself. To a certain extent it represents the essence without all the accessories.[52]

But one must make an important distinction between Hegel and Schopenhauer. With Hegel the Idea exists in an evolutionary sense, while with Schopenhauer the eternal Ideas exist outside of time, space, or causality. Schopenhauer goes further in another direction than Hegel. He divides the world into the Will as the thing itself and the Ideas as objectifications, i.e., the phenomena, copies, or images of the Will. The other arts cling only to the phenomena, and Ideas seek to be represented in it, while music is a direct objectification of the Will.

For music is such an immediate objectification and image of the entire Will, as is the world itself, and as are the Ideas, whose manifold appearances constitute the world of individual things. Music therefore is by no means like the other arts, an image of the Ideas, but rather an image of the Will, whose objectifications are the Ideas. Therefore, the efficacy of music is more powerful and penetrating than that of the other arts: for they speak only about shadows, but music about essence.[53]

The role of the artist is to discover the substance and meaning of the Ideas through "pure contemplation." The *raison d'être* of art lies in the acknowledgment of these Ideas, and its goal is the successful conveyance of them.

. . . the perception which examines and grasps the Ideas is art; the sole origin of art is the perception of the Ideas, its only aim the communication of this perception. . . . The essence of (artistic) genius lies in the ability of pure contemplation, which means the perception of Ideas. Genius seeks only the substance of the phenomenon, in which the Idea is expressed.[54]

With Schopenhauer one comes to the end of the idealistic tradition which influenced the early romantics and which had its origins in the writings of Herder.

CHAPTER III

BASIC PRINCIPLES OF SCHUMANN'S AESTHETICS

After having considered the intellectual climate surrounding Schumann, we will now discuss Schumann's basic aesthetic principles. It is unfortunate that he never completed a systematic treatise on aesthetics; that his ideas appear only in unpublished notes, which exist in manuscript form. These notes, early and incomplete, are grouped in various sets under the titles of *Ästhetische Fragmente und Aphorismen zur Ästhetik der Musik, Die Tonwelt, Aus dem Tagebuch der Hl. Cecilia*, and *Juniusabende und Julitage*. These fragments represent the only strict philosophic formalizing Schumann ever essayed, although interwoven in his criticisms, letters, and diaries are his ideas on aesthetics. It is questionable whether all that appears in the diary of a genius can be accepted as the truth, because a master will often color his thoughts for posterity. But Schumann, although he may have committed a few factual errors, in general relates events and ideas accurately. While Schumann admits the difficulties of the task, he purposes to be an accurate chronicler of his life.

It is certainly true . . . where feeling speaks the loudest, where the heart is filled with many rushing true dreams, there the cold hand cannot move the pen to note down those happy hours, during which one's dreams come true—I mean, to enter it in a cold, spiritless diary.[55]

One of the most common criticisms of Schumann, as found in Bekker's edition of Schumann's writings, is the conviction that he was not a philosopher.[56] Although Schumann is interested in all philosophy, he admits how unsure he is of the philosophic groundwork of his logic and perhaps that is why he never completed a treatise on aesthetics.

What I actually am, I do not yet clearly know. I believe I have imagination and which, moreover, no one will deny me. I am not a deep thinker; I can never logically continue the thread of thought which perhaps I have begun successfully. Whether I am a poet—since one can never become one—future generations should decide.[57]

A discussion of Schumann's aesthetics might consider first his remarks on tones and their properties. For him tones have a special intrinsic value, because in music they are abstractions which are not associated with images connected to life. Music, according to Schumann, is basically a language of the emotions, through which man is able to release his feelings.

Tones are the finest matter which our spirit contains, because for one thing, no graphic representation can be made of them. Also, they alone are the greatest gift of the deity, because they can be so easily understood and universally comprehended, notwithstanding their spiritual essence. . . . Music is the great invisible bond, which unites all souls, because in all spirits a harmonic accord prevails, and because in music harmony is the companionable union of tones. Music is the ability to express emotions audibly; it is the spiritual language of emotion, which is hidden more secretly than the soul; but one interwoven with the other dwells in the innermost region. The soul must first perceive pain and joy—just as at the clavier the keys must be touched before they sound; it is only then that the emotion communicates with the slumbering realm of tones. Thus music is the spiritual dissolution of our sensations. Not until we have experienced a pain or a joy in its entirety, does it excite us deeply—the spiritual realm of tones becomes alive, however, it becomes deeper and brighter in the soul. . . . Whoever possesses tones, does not need tears, both are equivalent—dissolved sensations of the soul.[58]

If music echoes the emotions, a moral influence is implied. "One can never listen to music and undertake something evil."[59] Music activates the deepest emotions man possesses, a sentiment which Schumann expresses in the *Juniusabende und Julitage.*

Tone as purely spiritual essence dwells entirely in man. And indeed: the simplest and most uncontrived combination of several tones will always make the deepest and most abiding impression on the soul . . .[60]

This pure outburst of feeling, unhampered by reflection, is what Schumann esteems in art.

Schumann believes that Nature, besides consoling and teaching the artist, also can illuminate his life; that the artist, through viewing the wonders of God, is able to perceive phenomena which otherwise would remain imperceptible. The artist's existence appears as the last remnant of a freer and earlier period in man's development, when man was closer to Nature.

So the poet lives a happy life; his eye becomes dark and insensitive in the noise of the day, but clear and serene it wakens in the solitude of Nature. The life of the poet seems to be the last residue from a happy

Arcadian time, when the childhood of man still walked in the harness of Nature.[61]

It is Schumann's opinion that one of the most important tasks an artist has is to raise the material above the mundane. "The greatest art in art itself is to spiritualize matter, so that everything material of it is forgotten." [62]

In temperament he is akin to the nature-philosophers who followed Jean Jacques Rousseau. These men attempt to reduce to an orderly system what the poets and musicians vaguely express. They believe that man and Nature are good. When man is close to Nature and expresses his true inner feelings, he is close to God.

Schumann believes that music is perceived by the senses in general terms, whereas the other arts are perceived in specific terms such as color, form, and size. Schumann's ideas on this subject bear a resemblance to those of Schopenhauer, who holds that music is a direct objectification of the Will, while the other arts are merely copies of the Ideas. As Schumann writes:

For the sense of sight every language has the greatest number of and most characteristic expressions. For the eye an object is light or dark, for the eye there are colors and forms, height and depth, breadth and length. It is a completely different matter with that which we perceive through hearing. Here we can distinguish only in terms of concord and discord. As soon as we want to embark on finer differentiations, we must call upon other senses for help.[63]

Although Schumann believes that music has the aforementioned advantages over the other arts, nevertheless he realizes that all the arts are interconnected. One of the prime requisites for a creative soul, according to Schumann, is for him to have an interest in and comprehension of all the arts. The medium for Schumann is of less importance than the ultimate result. The greater number of creative experiences an artist has undergone, the more valuable is his work. "Whoever understands Shakespeare and Jean Paul, will compose differently from one who has obtained his knowledge only from Marpurg, etc." [64] Because the fundamental nature of creativity is the same for the composer, painter and sculptor, the medium being the differing factor, their goals are similar, as are the standards applied in evaluating their accomplishments. Schumann eloquently expresses his theory of development through association with other arts in the following quotation from his *Denk-und Dichtbüchlein*, a notebook of short aphorisms.

The educated musician will be able to study a Raphael Madonna as advantageously as the painter a Mozart symphony. Moreover: for the sculptor the actor will become a quiet statue, and for the actor the works of the sculptor will become living figures; to the painter the poem becomes a picture, the musician transfers paintings into tones.[65]

The idea of the unification of the arts was one of the major themes of the romantic movement, and Schumann concludes that music and poetry have the same origin.

When we contemplate the height to which the sons of our time raise music, then it must be the more obvious that poetry and music spring from one and the same source. Or do you not think a Schiller, a Goethe, a Klopstock, and all the host of splendid singers of the German people have drawn their songs from the same holy well of enthusiasm, from which a Mozart, a Haydn, . . . called forth their harmonies? [66]

For a long time Schumann was undecided whether to become a poet or musician, but when he wanted to express his most poignant feelings, he knew instinctively that he must revert to music. He writes, "It is extraordinary that at the point where my emotions speak most strongly, I must give up being a poet." [67]

Some writers have misunderstood the implications of Schumann's poetic drive, by taking it too literally. What Schumann means by the word poet [Dichter] must be ascertained from his context. Usually he employs it in the literal sense to describe a man who dedicates his life to writing poetry; but also he uses the word in a more general sense to mean an artist or genius, as exemplified in the following quotation.

The poet's eye is the most beautiful and richest; I do not take objects as they are, but just as I perceive them subjectively within me, and so one lives more easily and freely. The more restricted the world is from the outside, the more it grows through fantasy on the inside.[68]

Schumann believes that the poet stands above the ordinary course of life and extracts its quintessence. His power of contemplative perception is one of his greatest gifts, because he has the ability to grasp the core and disregard the superficial.

Poetry is the bright crystal, in which the spiritual life of generations is mirrored purely and clearly; the glittering prism which reflects all colors etherealized in a more beautiful and purer light. . . . The poet stands above his locale; he looks yearningly to the distant light of the stars and opens the wings of his soul; and when the seventy minutes, which we call years, are struck, he raises himself and rising ignites himself like a phoenix, and the ashes of his feathers fall back and his

27

unveiled soul comes, without earthly connections (?) and pure as a tone, into the heavens.[69]

As music and poetry are inextricably blended, with music possessing the greater emotional and expressive power, so on another plane a similar relationship exists between feeling and intellect. A significant theme which predominated in much nineteenth century romantic literature was the necessity for man to trust his emotions. This was a reflection of the movement which shunned reason as a guiding force in life and wanted emotion to perform a larger role.[70]

As a child, Schumann schooled himself to regard passion as a sublime sentiment which was capable of transfiguring both its subject and object; as an artist he reacts similarly, because he believes emotion to lie at the core of art. For Schumann, personal emotion is reflected in his artistic creation, and he writes to his mother that the purest emotions are the finest. "God grant me that I remain only thoroughly strong, modest, sturdy and temperate. The natural, pure flame is always the most beautiful and most warming." [71] Schumann further extols emotion by stating that: "Ideas or emotions, that is something different; we are all more creatures of emotion than we believe." [72]

Schumann's biography indicates that he lacked formal musical training. The young Schumann showed great interest in music, and his father fostered this proclivity by sending him at the age of six to Baccalaureus Kuntzsch, a local school teacher, for piano lessons. Although Kuntzsch lacked theoretical training, he encouraged the creativity in young Schumann, who showed a remarkable talent for composition even at the age of twelve. Schumann's father desired to send him to Carl Maria von Weber for serious instruction in music, but the plan was never carried out. On the death of his father in 1826, Schumann was coerced into going to Leipzig to study law. However, he never applied himself to this, and continued to be interested only in music. It was in Leipzig that he met Friedrich Wieck, who taught him piano. However, it was not until he made the acquaintance of Heinrich Dorn in June, 1831 that he undertook to study the theoretical aspects of music.

In view of his lack of formal musical training, it is perhaps understandable that Schumann mistrusts theoretical analysis, often complains about theory, and wishes he had enough talent to be able to bypass the burdensome matter.

To theory everything is veiled. . . . Pure unfettered, freely moving Nature poeticized more beautifully, because at that time there were no theories. . . . Above all, it is bad that we think more than we feel. . . . Philosophy may remain cold.[73]

After studying Gottfried Weber's book, *Versuch einer geordneten Theorie der Tonsetzkunst,* Schumann writes:

Evening, theory by Weber. Oh this theory, this whole theory! If only I were a genius, so that I could kill all dullards with it; would I not like to load it all in a cannon and shoot someone dead with it! [74]

He recognizes inspiration's ephemeral nature and the speed with which it vanishes as soon as a state of consciousness is attained. "The mind errs, the soul does not." [75] The true origin of conception occurs in a state of either complete passivity or unconscious activity of the mind.

In man dwells a great awesome something, . . . we feel it at sunset or at the sound of soft tones. Why does the dream and happiness always vanish for me at the beginning of consciousness? To know is little, to feel is more and to desire is the most. He who wants to experience this will get to know himself best.[76]

A corollary of this principle is that a composer must write with swiftness and surety in order to capture fleeting sensations.

Avoid, above all, any subsequent contemplation, rather make the conception a fact immediately. Agility is the greatest mastery, is this not the case with Mozart, Goethe, Schiller? [77]

According to Schumann, a great artistic creation does not necessarily emerge from a composer who first makes an outline of his work and then weighs all the pertinent impressions which have occurred to him. Rather it springs from the hidden depths of imagination.

The process which makes the composer choose between this or that fundamental key to express his emotions, is as inexplicable as the creation of the genius itself, which, along with the idea, offers the form, the vessel, which securely encloses the idea.[78]

Schumann's definition of a genius and the qualities which the genius possesses are an important part of Schumann's aesthetics. Schumann describes genius in the following terms: "Genius [*Genialität*] in art and eye does not include merely the idea of the beautiful and lofty, but the association of all ideas expressed in one individual." [79]

Schumann's thoughts on the creative genius may be inferred

29

from his ideas on creativity. A genius has complete freedom to express his feelings, a liberty which is denied others, although he must obey rules and has not the license to compose any way he fancies. An inner coherence must be present in a composition. The genius, in his attempt to realize his creative impulses, is given freedom only to break pedantic rules which may hinder him.

Although society does not always recognize the genius, Schumann claims that the creative spirit is responsible for the progress made in art.

. . . one would be lost in displeasure, if in the ordinary hustle and bustle of the day a young hero did not once again suddenly appear, a true representative of artistic interests, vigorously and courageously making his way. Also, he must not complain about the indifference of the world, so strongly does true talent seize the time from head to foot.[80]

Schumann recognizes the difficulty in explaining the "secret powers of creative ability",[81] although he trusts this inexplicable force. He evokes it often in his diaries by asking it not to forsake him, for example:

Before Thee my Genius, I sink! Let me look into the beautiful world and carry me farther. Thanks to my good Genius, who wants to take me under his wings. Do not forsake me! God protect me, my Genius, and never deceive me.[82]

Schumann's conception of an aristocracy of talent is centered around those who are endowed with the sacred gift. No one may be admitted to the elite circle of men, who does not possess fantasy, feeling, and imagination [Phantasie, Gemüt, Geist]. Schumann looks upon the formation of such a society, which had its practical realization in the formation of the Davidsbund, as a progressive move in the understanding of art.

An advance of our art would occur first with an advance of artists toward an aristocracy of the mind, the statutes of which do not merely demand knowledge of the bare mechanics . . . and according to which no one would be admitted who is not sufficiently talented to achieve for himself what he expects of others, . . . in order to bring about an epoch of a higher level of general musical culture.[83]

Schumann believes that artists should be the ones chosen to judge each other's works, an idea which is derived from the reciprocal relationship existing between geniuses. It has been shown that Schumann uses the word "poet" in a literal and general sense. He employs the word "artist" similarly. For Schu-

30

mann, a critic also must be an artist. But when he uses the word "artist", he is not restricting it to a literal meaning, embracing only the practicing artist. Rather, he also includes those artistic people who have an understanding of the creative genius, although they themselves may not create art. Indeed, a higher level of culture would contain genuine art lovers and connoisseurs as well as creative artists.

No one can be a judge who is not also an artist. But it should not pass unnoticed what those who judge have done for the history of art, although they were not exactly practicing artists.[84]

Furthermore, the artist must acknowledge his contemporaries. ". . . an artist who refuses to recognize the strivings of his better contemporaries would have to be included in the number of the lost ones." [85]

One of the basic questions which occupied Schumann's mind is the distinction between the creating genius and the working talent. This was a problem which concerned many of the eighteenth and early nineteenth century philosophers.[86] In Schumann's discussion of the qualities which constitute talent, genius comes spontaneously, whereas talent progresses slowly. This means that a creative person may produce an acceptable composition with intensive work; but a genius can create his masterpiece not only in a more concentrated period of time, but also with a flair, because he has the gift of inspiration. The genius envisions the whole in a moment. Schumann describes the talented man (the composer J. J. H. Verhulst) in the following terms:

Talents of his kind, indeed, do not advance rapidly, but with so much the safer strides; diligence, observation, association with masters, likewise public encouragement also helped. And so there is no doubt at all, that the young tree will bear ever more mature and richer fruit from year to year.[87]

Although Schumann does not exclude the possibility of a capable person creating a work of art, he regrets the distribution of talent, and grieves about the capriciousness with which nature distributes her gifts.

To this one she offers character, but inflexibility, to that one inventiveness, but carelessness; to another the urge for acclaim, but no persistence, to still another poetic thoughts, but no ability to handle them; to many something, to most, little.[88]

The mere knowledge of art does not imply an ability to create. The cleavage which exists between knowing and creating is reconciled only after tedious conflicts. ". . . but of course there is an immense abyss between knowledge and creation, and often it is only after hard struggles that a connecting bridge arises." [89] Any person endowed with a fertile talent has an obligation to produce.

Although Schumann claims that a man who is merely gifted may possess certain qualities, it is impossible for him to rise to great heights, because his efforts result only in pedantic busy work. A genius is able to realize his ideals and haughtily mocks his inferiors. It is unfortunate when the followers of a creative mind attempt to imitate their master, because they are always unsuccessful.

Only in order to win the pearl does one visit the dangerous depths of the sea. This is precisely the curse of talent, that even though it progresses and accomplishes more securely and continuously, it finally must stop at the boundary of its goal, while genius easily floats at the summit of the ideal and smilingly looks about from above.[90]

In view of the two levels of creativity which Schumann acknowledges, it is understandable that he would assign a specific language to each level—an earthly one spoken by the talented, and a spiritual one by the genius. The origin of the genius' language is unknown and inexplicable.

There are two languages of art, the common earthly one which the majority of the disciples of art learn to speak in school with diligence and good will, and the higher one, the celestial one, which mocks the most persistent studies, and to which men must be born. The lower language is a canal which, in a straight line, follows a regulated but only forced path; the higher is a forest current which roaringly breaks out of the neighborhood of the clouds. One does not know from where it comes or to where it goes; it flows, as Klopstock says, "strong and full of thoughts". The prophets spoke this language, and it is also the language of artists; for artists are prophets.[91]

According to Schumann's conception of the artist's role in society, the creative spirit must perceive Nature's teachings and present them to the public. In so doing, he finds joyful fulfillment.

In Nature the soul learns to pray best and to consecrate all gifts which the higher Being gave us. Nature is the great unfolded handkerchief of God, embroidered with His eternal name, on which man can dry all his tears of pain, but also tear of joy.[92]

Schumann contends that an artist must not disassociate himself from the outside world, because the world is one of his greatest sources of inspiration.

The artist should partake of life; in a study ideas seldom develop. Exterior circumstances have unlimited influence. . . . Protect yourself from onesidedness, then you will live three times as long in the world. . . . The artist must keep an equilibrium with the outside world, otherwise he goes down, . . .[93]

Although a creative spirit is dissatisfied with the earthly part of life, because the higher he strives, the more removed he is from his goal, still, according to Schumann, he must live with society and attempt to perceive its pulse. It is at these moments, when the poet reflects the character of those surrounding him, and they understand him, that great art is produced.

The true periods of poetry are those in which poet and people become a unity, merge into a whole, when the interest of the former is so closely united with the latter, that one can see reflected in the poet the character of the people, and vice versa, from the words of the poet one can come to conclusions regarding the character of the nation.[94]

At times, however, Schumann realizes that he is out of focus with his society. By nature, Schumann was retiring and inarticulate with his contemporaries. Preferring contemplation, he would rather write than talk. Because of this, he is compelled to defend the benefits of solitude. For Schumann, the source of solitude lies within ourselves; it is not simply a physical circumstance, although solitude is more easily achieved when one is detached from his surroundings. Furthermore, solitude does not mean simply a sense of being alone, but rather a feeling of self-sufficiency and independence of mind.

Solitude is communication with ourselves; it is [the state of] being removed from all outside impressions which the world exerts upon us. . . . It may be called the active condition of the soul combined with passivity of the body. . . . They are, as the Frenchmen Montaigne says, precisely the greater minds who feel most alone in society, and in solitude they feel most occupied;[95] but solitude is produced in our innermost self. We can enjoy its presence to the greatest advantage when we are away from the noise of the world.[96]

A letter to his friend Gisbert Rosen, dated June, 1828, contains an example of this ambivalent attitude toward society.

Ah, a world *without* people, what would it be? An eternal cemetery —a mortal sleep without dreams, a nature without flowers and without spring, a dead peep-show without figures—but yet, this peopled world, what is it? A monstrous graveyard of sunken dreams—a garden with cypress trees and weeping willows, a mute peep-show with weeping figures.[97]

Perhaps Schumann sees in the conflict between the need for both the world and solitude a reflection of the Hegelian dialectic of thesis and antithesis. From these contradictory impulses arose a synthesis, of great music and clear insight into the nature of art and its creation.

Schumann's romanticism is seen clearly in several of his aesthetic principles. For example, he contends that a romantic composer must be a poetic musician. "The romantic element, however, does not lie in the figures and forms; it will be present anyhow, if the composer is a poet at all." [98]

Secondly, according to Schumann, the romantic era is not a revolutionary one, but rather an outgrowth of the previous century. He applies this principle to musicians:

If they do not understand some of the present creations and many others of the future, since their insight into periods of transition is lacking, it is their fault. The new so-called romantic school did not grow out of nothing; everything has its good reason.[99]

This is a noteworthy quotation because it displays Schumann's cognizance of another approach to art. He recognizes that art, although it may differ from the past, is still related to it. At various times throughout his life Schumann labeled himself a classicist, although if one examines the characteristics which distinguish him, he is in fact a romanticist. He has a subjective outlook; he requires a fusion of poetry and music; he views the arts as related to life; he desires to make the momentary permanent; and he places emotion above form.

One of the more obvious differences between a classic and a romantic is shown in the former's ability to stand above his work, while the latter is inextricably involved within it. But because Schumann admits to a dualism in his personality on one level, i.e., poet versus musician, it is not surprising to discover it on another, i.e., in his desire to remain a member of both movements, classic and romantic. Although he respects Liszt and Wagner, he never adopts their revolutionary mode of expression in musical composition.

The piano music of Robert Schumann exhibits the aesthetic principles which have been presented in this chapter. First of all, Schumann stresses the importance of tone as the raw material of music. In examining the *Allegro*, Opus 8, one finds at the beginning isolated tones placed between arpeggiations of chords, with a stress on sound for its own sake (Example 1, p. 35). Midway through the piece Schumann again employs similar tones, com-

Example Number 1. Robert Schumann, Allegro,
Opus 8, Volume 1, p. 169.

Allegro

plete in themselves, separated by arpeggiated chords (Example 2, p. 37).

Because of the incorporeal nature of tones, music is particularly suited for the expression of the emotions. Schumann recognizes the importance of pure emotion in his piano music. He captures different emotional moods in *Kinderszenen*, which is unified by a juxtaposition of emotions within a significant framework of unity, variety, and balance.

Moreover, the emotions found in *Kinderszenen* are presented directly, a corollary of the above idea. For example, "Glückes genug" can be seen as an attempt by Schumann to present a single emotion in its purest state. Often the listener has the impression that the pieces in *Kinderszenen* are a result of fleeting inspiration, an observation which is supported by the succinctness and brevity of each individual piece. The selection "Fast zu ernst" is an example of Schumann's attempt to present a single emotion directly. In "Fürchtenmachen", the emotions of suspense and terror are intertwined, forming a single scene.

Because of its ethereal nature, music has a quality of strangeness. This element of obscurity is also present in Schumann's piano works. The *Phantasiestücke*, Opus 12, contain pieces which are dark in nature. "Des Abends", "In der Nacht", and "Traumes-Wirren" conjure up mysterious and fantastic images, which were such an integral part of the romantic spirit. Even the title of the collection, *Nachtstücke*, exhibits a concern with the obscure.

In spite of Schumann's contention that the depiction of darkness and mystery is found more in music than in the other arts, he realizes that all the arts are interconnected. In fact, this principle of his aesthetics is most influential in the composition of his piano music. A reflection of his attempt to relate the arts lies in his use of early songs in some of his later piano works. He incorporates the song "An Anna II" in the second movement of the *Sonata in F minor*, "Im Herbste" in the *Sonata in G minor*, and "Der Hirtenknabe" in the "Intermezzo", Opus 4, Number 4.

He is especially motivated by the connection of poetry and music. *Papillons* is inspired by the masked ball in Jean Paul's novel *Flegeljahre*; *Kreisleriana* is influenced by E. T. A. Hoffmann's character Kapellmeister Kreisler. Schumann assumes that his listeners will be familiar with the literary allusions which he uses to deepen the meaning of his music. Schumann moves from a more obscure connection between literature and music as seen in *Papillons*, which is related to the ending of a novel, to the closer

Example Number 2. Robert Schumann, Allegro, Opus 8, Volume 1, p. 175.

connection found in *Kreisleriana*, which is based on a fictitious person. The title *Papillons* is not obviously related to Jean Paul's novel, whereas the name *Kreisleriana* more directly suggests Kapellmeister Kreisler. Finally, he moves even closer by incorporating poetry in the score. In the "Intermezzo", Opus 4, Number 2, Schumann writes above the music the first line of the song which Gretchen sings at the spinning wheel in *Faust* (Example 3, p. 39). In the *Davidsbündlertänze*, he quotes an old poem which speaks of uniting happiness and sorrow, which correspond to the two sides of Schumann's nature (Example 4, p. 40).

> In all and every time
> Pleasure and pain are linked;
> Stay pious in pleasure and be
> Ready for sorrow with courage.

This poem is particularly applicable to the first edition of the *Davidsbündlertänze*, because most of the dances are marked with either "F.", "E.", or "F. and E.", the abbreviations of Schumann's pseudonyms, Florestan and Eusebius.

In the *Phantasie*, Schumann uses a few lines of Friedrich Schlegel to set the mood of the piece (Example 5, p. 41).

> Through all sounds resounds
> In the colored earthly dream
> A quiet sound drawn
> For him, who secretly listens.

Schlegel's poem reflects the Hegelian Idea of an underlying spirit at the core of reality. The particular sounds which a person hears are only a reflection, as it were, of the Ideal Sound. He who secretly listens will understand that the Ideal Sound is at the center of the imagination (*Phantasie*) which produces the musical tones. It is quite probably that the person Schumann means is Beethoven, in whose honor the *Phantasie* originally was written; perhaps also Liszt, as interpreter or recreator, to whom the work is dedicated. Moreover, the very title, *Phantasie*, links the piece to those who exercise imagination, and, on a higher level, to the Ideal Sound as the source of musical imagination.

From observing the various media of art, Schumann comes to believe that emotion is at the core of all art. Indeed, Schumann considers emotion more important than intellect, and consequently his piano compositions reflect the emphasis. In this he is in the mainstream of romantic aesthetics. As with Wordsworth, Schumann is not governed by the more classic principles of form,

Example Number 3. Robert Schumann, <u>Intermezzi</u>,
Opus 4, Number 2, Volume 1, p. 58.

Example Number 4. Robert Schumann, Davidsbündlertänze,
Opus 6, Volume 1, p. 105.

Davidsbündlertänze
Davidsbündler-Dances   Danses de Davidsbündler

Alter Spruch
In all und jeder Zeit
Verknüpft sich Lust und Leid:
Bleibt fromm in Lust und seid
Dem Leid mit Mut bereit

Walther von Goethe zugeeignet

Erste Ausgabe
First edition
Première Edition

Robert Schumann, Op. 6
(1837)

*)Clara Wieck

40

Example Number 5. Robert Schumann, Phantasie,
Opus 17, Volume 3, p. 90.

Phantasie
Fantasia   Fantaisie

Franz Liszt gewidmet

Motto:
Durch alle Töne tönet
Im bunten Erdentraum
Ein leiser Ton gezogen
Für den,der heimlich lauschet.
Fr. Schlegel

Robert Schumann, Op. 17
(1836)

Durchaus fantastisch und leidenschaftlich vorzutragen M.M. ♩=80
Sempre fantasticamente ed appassionatamente

41

but rather shapes the form to fit his ideas. *Carnaval*, which is held together by such technical devices as a *soggetto cavato*, keys with signatures from two to five flats, and dance rhythms, is unified also by the various emotions and personages which it presents, the idea of a masked ball, and the mood of carnival time. The *Novelletten* are, in a certain sense, a shifting kaleidoscope of emotions, rather than a tightly organized series of pieces. They are held together by an emotional framework and a series of changing tonalities. The piece can be viewed as the emotional outpouring of a romantic soul, rather than a carefully chiseled work of art. Often a particular mood will act as the unifying factor, as found in *Faschingsschwank aus Wien*, which is held together by the spirit of carnival time. Schumann deepens the impression by quoting the French national anthem as a joke, and by employing dance rhythms and song textures throughout.

Because of his romantic ideas about the nature of the creative process, Schumann, from 1830 to 1840, places little reliance on musical theory. Although Schumann uses such contrapuntal techniques as imitation, canon, and stretto, he does not write strict canons or fugues. He trusts in the fleeting moods of his own emotion to inspire him.

Schumann's emphasis on emotion and spontaneity forms the basis of his conception of a creative genius. One of the factors that greatly influenced Schumann's piano music is his belief in the existence of an elite circle of geniuses who alone can criticize and truly understand each other's work. For example, the *Davidsbündlertänze* are a reflection of the *Davidsbund*, Schumann's semi-fictitious organization which united many of the progressive musicians of the first half of the nineteenth century. The "Marche des 'Davidsbündler' contre les Philistins" in *Carnaval* also exemplifies the idea. Two of the most important members of the *Davidsbund* are Florestan and Eusebius, who represent the two conflicting sides of Schumann's personality. They are characterized musically in the *Davidsbündlertänze*, as well as in *Carnaval*.

Despite the fact that Schumann holds to the conception of an aristocracy of talent, he always keeps in mind the audience which will hear his music. Through his art he hopes to convey the deep emotions he experienced in his own soul. An example of the desire to present his art to society is the *Phantasie*, Opus 17, which was written to commemorate the dedication of a statue of Beethoven in Bonn.

At the same time, however, it was shown that Schumann values solitude highly. The apparent contradiction between Schumann's need for society and his desire for solitude is part of Schumann's double nature. The feeling of loneliness and isolation is conveyed well in the portrait of "Eusebius" in *Carnaval*, which is slow, melancholy, and withdrawn. In the piece "Der Dichter Spricht" from *Kinderszenen*, the same impression is created through the slow tempo, the soft dynamic range, and the hymn-like sections which surround a central recitative.

The last principle of Schumann's aesthetics to be discussed in this chapter is his firm belief that music spiritualizes matter. Following the Hegelian view of the artist, Schumann acts as the spokesman of God, by revealing through his art a part of the obscure reality which underlies appearances. Schumann translates the basic matter of reality into spiritual terms that can be assimilated by the human soul. This crucial principle pervades all of Schumann's piano music.

We have shown that Schumann's aesthetic principles are strongly romantic. However, his complex personality cannot easily be categorized. Schumann elevates the value of subjectivity to a norm, by recognizing the existence of a subjective element at the center of all creativity, and by trying to capture and amalgamate the different sides of his personality in his compositions. The conflict takes the form of a battle within himself—Florestan versus Eusebius. The subjectivity of Schumann leads to an oscillation between the outer world of sense and experience and the inner world of ideas and emotions.

CHAPTER IV

SCHUMANN'S VIEWS ON CRITICISM

To understand Schumann's musical criticisms and their underlying theories requires a comprehension of the trends and aims of
romantic criticism. The romantic conception of criticism exists as
a reconstructive process. This means that the critic, in attempting
to evaluate a work of art, endeavors to recreate the artist's ideas
in his own language. Because only geniuses understand each other's work, only a genius can criticize another. This theme is
linked with the conception of an aristocracy of talent; and thus
dilettantes who do not actively participate in the creative process
are unable to assess the works of artists. The true critic, on the
other hand, understands the inner nature of art because he is
himself an artist, although he may not be a practicing one.

To a certain extent the romantic is a born translator and critic.
As translator, he interprets nature, art and the past in terms understandable to his contemporaries. As critic, he judges the work
of others by utilizing his innate yearning to reflect. The conception of a critic's function differed at various times in history.
There is, for example, William Hazlitt (1778-1830), who developed a theory of "impressionistic" criticism; that is, his critical
judgment is based on the impression a work makes on him rather
than on objective standards. Hazlitt's reliance on his emotional
response to art makes him conceive the task of criticism as com-
municating these feelings.

I say what I think; I think what I feel. I cannot help receiving certain
impressions from things; and I have sufficient courage to declare
(somewhat abruptly) what they are.[100]

Hazlitt's stress on personal criticism is typically romantic.
However, he differs from some of the romantics in that he relies
more on his own impressions of the work, than on an attempt to
identify himself with the poet. The need for identification is expressed by Ugo Foscolo (1778-1827), an Italian romantic writer
who says:

To develop the beauties of a poem the critic must go through the same reasonings and judgments which ultimately determined the poet to write as he has done. But such a critic would be a poet.[101]

A consideration of the classical critics in Germany reveals definite roots for the ideas which appear in the nineteenth century. Gotthold Ephraim Lessing (1729-1781) writes: "Not every critic is a genius, but every genius is a born critic. He has the proof of all rules within himself." [102] Johann Wolfgang von Goethe (1749-1832) and Herder are believers in sympathetic criticism; their aim is to "penetrate the sense and the intentions of the author." [103] As Goethe writes:

Some of my well-wishing readers have told me for a long time that instead of expressing a judgment on books, I describe the influence which they have had on me. And at bottom this is the way all readers criticize, even if they do not communicate an opinion and formulate ideas about it to the public.[104]

Goethe reflects the romantic attitude in his critical subjectivity; but he also exhibits a similarity to Hazlitt, in that Goethe does not primarily stress the reproduction of an art object as the aim of a critic. The work of late eighteenth century writers such as Hazlitt, Lessing, and the early Goethe foreshadows later ideas on criticism.

Friedrich Schlegel (1772-1829) is one of the true romantic critics. For him the aim of criticism is:

. . . to give us a reflection of the work itself, to communicate its peculiar spirit, to present the pure impression in such a way that the form of the presentation verifies the artistic citizenship of its author: not merely a poem about a poem, in order to dazzle for the moment; not merely the impression which the work has made yesterday or makes today on this or that person; but that which it should always make on all educated people.[105]

He wanders from the mainstream of romantic thought in his refusal to recognize historical relativism, which is an integral part of the Hegelian dialectic. Schlegel postulates the universality of an impression by implying an absolute set of standards for evaluating, and speaks of the whole and the necessity of gaining the spirit, tone, and general character of a work. The critic must not only perceptively reconstruct, but also must characterize the work's subtler peculiarities.

And it can be said that one has understood a work and a mind only if one can reconstruct its course and structure. Now this profound understanding which, if expressed in definite words is called characterization, is the actual business and inner essence of criticism.[106]

According to Friedrich Schlegel:

Characterization requires (1) geography, as it were. . . . (2) a spiritual and aesthetic architectonics of the work, its essence, its tone; and finally (3) the psychological genesis, the origin of its motivation through laws and conditions of human nature.[107]

The subjective element which is found in Goethe and Hazlitt is expanded by August Schlegel (1767-1845), who combines objective standards with the critic's personal reactions. The critic aspires to raise the less talented to his own point of view. His *Dramatische Vorträge* include an expression of the desire for a:

. . . universality of the spirit, i.e., . . . flexibility which enables us, by renouncing personal predilection and blind habit, to transfer ourselves into the peculiarities of other nations and ages, to feel them, as it were, from their own center.[108]

August Schlegel believes that criticism should exhibit empathy with the ideals of the artist, which implies a requisite creative ability, enabling the critic to understand the artist's endeavors. Furthermore, Schlegel emphasizes the unity of a work of art. "A beautiful whole can never be pieced together from beautiful parts; the whole must first be posited absolutely and then the particular evolved from it." [109]

These ideas are enlarged upon by Wackenroder and Novalis (Friedrich von Hardenberg) (1772-1801). Wackenroder recognizes the gulf which divides the artist from the critic; the critic can discover only external facts about the creative process, but is unable to comprehend how it functions.

Whoever with the divining rod of searching understanding wants to discover what can be felt only from inside, will eternally discover only thoughts about feeling and never the feeling itself. An eternal hostile gulf is fixed between the feeling heart and the investigations of research. Thus feeling can, after all, be grasped and understood only by feeling.[110]

The culmination of the romantic attitude toward criticism lies in the admission by Novalis of the existence of "productive criticism", which is the ability to reproduce the object under close examination. To a certain extent, the critic's function is abolished, because he becomes a poet. One should:

Censure nothing human. Everything is good, but not everywhere, but not always, but not for everybody. That is the case with criticism. When judging poems, e.g., one should take care more to censure what is, strictly speaking, a real artistic mistake, a false tone in every

46

connection. One should assign to every poem, as exactly as possible, its precinct, and that is enough criticism for the folly of its author.[111]

In addition to the influence of other romantic critics, Schumann also relies on his aesthetics, as a basis for his criticism. Schumann is in tune with the main currents of romantic criticism; he considers the critic's main function a reconstructive one. Schumann believes that critics are necessary for a life of art; as far as Schumann can tell there is no period in which artists and critics fail to be of mutual assistance in the development of a cultural life.

Beware Eusebius, of underestimating dilettantism (in the better sense), [which is] inseparable from a life of art. For the expression "no artist, no connoisseur" must be considered a half-truth, as long as a period cannot be shown in which art has flowered without that reciprocal action.[112]

The inability of critics to evaluate music competently disturbs Schumann. This failure is due in part to the lack of contact between musician and critic. Schumann finds that musicians are incapable of verbalizing their ideas, and those who write criticism fail to understand the work of the musician. Thus both sides are responsible for the gulf which exists between composer and critic.

The arts should be cultivated only by the talented. . . . The language of benevolence in musical criticism would be self-explanatory, if it always could be directed to the talented. So war often becomes necessary. The musical polemic still offers an enormous field; this would be because only a few musicians write well and most writers are no true musicians; neither rightly knows how to deal with the matter. Therefore, musical struggles end mostly with mutual retreat or with an embrace.[113]

Schumann believes that critics often ask the composer questions which defy verbal explanations. In attempting to reply, the composer is not understood. Schumann hopes for an era when music will speak for itself, and the terms "composer" and "critic" will be synonymous.

For critics always want to know what the composers themselves cannot tell them, and critics understand scarcely ten per cent of that which they criticize. Oh Heaven, when will the time finally come, when we are asked no longer what we intend to express with our divine compositions! Look for the fifths, and leave us in peace.[114]

Schumann finds a similar gulf between himself and the average person. As an individual Schumann feels he is an outsider, a belief

47

which becomes intensified during his later years. The man of average taste, the Philistine, lacks understanding or sympathy for music. He would prefer the age of powdered wigs [*Zopfzeit*], which flourished with the ascendance of rationalism during the seventeenth and eighteenth centuries. "The Philistine jumbles everything together. What is not clear to him, he calls romantic. What he understands infuses him with hope for a return to the *ancien regime* [*Zopfzeit*]; then he is cheered up." [115]

Although Schumann admits the difficulties involved in expressing himself through criticism, he hopes that his critical writings will serve as a guide for the understanding of his own works.

I am not concerned in gaining, as it were, treasures thereby; I would like to leave behind a remembrance of myself, . . . the commentary [*Text*] to my productive creation.[116]

Requested to do so by many of my friends, I have compiled my literary works on music and on musical conditions of the immediate past, revised [them] and added new ones; and what appeared scattered and for the most part without my signature in the various issues of the *Neue Zeitschrift für Musik*, I would like to have appear in book form as a remembrance of me.[117]

Schumann asks other critics to judge his compositions by the same standards which he employs to evaluate the works of others. They should not disapprove of his work, but rather attempt to understand his aim. He is willing to accept criticism, positive or negative, but he must sense that the critic has tried to view his work sympathetically. He states this idea in a letter to Julius Rietz, dated November 1, 1848.

My aim, as you will believe me, [judging] from my previous efforts in art, is not to force from you or from anyone else unconditional praise, enthusiasm about my work. No, I wish only this, that the one in whose hands to a great extent lies the success of such laborious work will approach it with that same artistic sympathy, . . . In other words, criticism I can bear, but Mr. Music Director, I shall not permit my work to be looked down upon.[118]

By what standards should a critic judge a composition? In Schumann's opinion a critic can read extensively about the genesis of a composition and analyze it, but the best explanation lies in the music itself.

It occurred to me again that one is certainly never finished with Bach; that he will always become more profound, the more one listens to him. . . . The best illustration and explanation of his works always remains the living one, through the means of the music itself.[119]

Above all, the critic must appreciate the composition as a unit, although he may discover beauty in separate parts.

It is inadmissible to want to measure a whole life according to one single deed. . . . Dissect a Beethoven symphony which is unfamiliar to you, and see whether a most beautiful idea, torn out of it, has an effect by itself. More than in the works of the pictorial arts, where the single torso can identify a master, in music the interrelation, the totality, means everything, on a small scale as on a large.[120]

Furthermore, the critic must take into account the direction of his own development in relation to that of the composer. In a letter to Edward Krueger, June 14, 1839, Schumann writes that because he can not sympathize completely with Krueger's style of composing, he can not adequately evaluate its worth.

It is very difficult for me to judge your compositions, because I go in such a different direction; and only the very best excites me, nearly all of Bach, Beethoven mostly in his later works. Do not, therefore, consider me unfair. I began to compose immediately, and the simply lyrical did not satisfy me even in my early years. So I soon arrived at Beethoven, soon at Bach; books and surroundings, inner as well as outer experiences also affected me.[121]

For Schumann, the overall impression of a work must be clear to the unsophisticated listeners. If the effect of the piece on the listener is clear, then he can speak in terms of whether or not a work of art appeals to him.

The impression of a piece must not be dubious—if it is, then the uneducated says, it pleases me or it does not. . . . And who demands from a listener, when a piece is played for him for the first time, that he dissect it right into the mechanical or harmonic parts? [122]

However, the first impression of a work is not sufficient for proper criticism. In Schumann's opinion a competent review requires maturity.

The more mature the judgment, the more simply and modestly will it express itself. Only he, who by tenfold repetition, by conscientious comparison, in long continued self-denial, has pursued the phenomena, knows how slowly our knowledge increases, how slowly our judgment purifies itself, and how cautious, therefore, we must be in our statements. Somewhere I read [that] "without the most manifold experience and guiding knowledge [Leitkenntnisse] we are, although with open eyes, blind to a work of art".[123]

With maturity, the critic comes to realize that every artist only approaches the goal he is striving to achieve, a limitation the critic should realize and take into consideration when he is evaluating a work.

However, all aspirations in art are approximate, no work of art is absolutely perfect—no tone of the voice, no sound of speech, no movement of the body, no line of the painter.[124]

Not only do critics, according to Schumann, often misjudge a work by not realizing the gulf between a masterpiece and the creator's conception, but also they make snap judgments on the basis of first impressions. This occurs in connection with modern works, which are often badly reviewed. Because Schumann is progressive, he appreciates young composers who write in a modern idiom, and he takes pains to bring them to the attention of the public. Most critics, Schumann believes, are not progressive. They model their ideas on old-fashioned standards, which do not reflect new currents of thought.

It seems to me much more important that the critic interpose with strength and discretion in the new activity of new spirits, rather than busy himself trivially with relics of old passions. Noble withdrawal or pedantic clinging to ancient relics [Zopf], or dreaming about youthful love is worthless and useless. Time moves on, and one must move on with it.[125]

On the other hand, Schumann cautions the listener not to be overwhelmed by novel effects. "The unusual astonishes us when we are close to it, but the power of the moment always prevents us from distinguishing between cause and effect. With distance, consciousness returns." [126]

After having examined the failings Schumann ascribes to contemporary critics, one might investigate Schumann as a critic and see whether he abides by his own principles. His aim is to act as a mediator between the artist and the public, and to lessen the gulf between the musician and the critic.

His main purpose as a critic has as much an instructive as artistic aim. He feels the dawn of a new age with the appearance of romantic composers on the scene, he seeks to educate the public, and he seldom pays attention to what is fashionable in music, but rather to the intrinsic worth of compositions. Armed with his principles and ideas, he fights against mediocrity. Although he is a link in the development of a musical style between Beethoven and Brahms, he is not intolerant of Liszt and Wagner. Schumann is conscious of his goal and believes it is his aim ". . . to prepare a new poetic era, to help accelerate it." [127]

Because Schumann had both musical and literary talents, it was fortunate for him to be able to combine these abilities so successfully in the role of music critic. Dissatisfied with the state of criticism, Schumann and his friends established the *Neue Zeitschrift für Musik* and wrote many articles for it. Although Schumann enjoyed his life as a critic, any obstacle which tended to interrupt his musical development was fated to be discarded. As he writes to Heinrich Dorn, his counterpoint teacher and friend, in April, 1839:

With the *Zeitschrift*, meanwhile, many an event of my inner and outer life will have been made known to you. Basically I am very happy in my sphere of activity; but if only I could throw away the journal completely, live completely as an artist for music, not have to occupy myself with so many trivialities, which editorial work necessarily requires; only then would I be completely at home, within myself and within the world. Perhaps the future still will bring this, and then there will be only symphonies by me to be edited and heard.[128]

In spite of his desire to devote himself entirely to composition, Schumann maintained his position with the *Neue Zeitschrift für Musik* until July, 1844. Then, for reasons of health, he finally relinquished it. Schumann regretted giving up the position, because he realized the deplorable state of nineteenth century music criticism, and consequently he remained in an advisory capacity.

As a critic, one of Schumann's most noteworthy qualities lies in the encouragement he gives to young composers. For example, in evaluating Sterndale Bennett's work, he praises ". . . this early developed artist's hand, . . . calm arrangement, . . . cohesion of the whole, . . . pleasing sound of language, purity of thought." [129]

Schumann is especially kind to young composers, because he realizes the obstacles which lie before them, and the reluctance with which listeners accept them. After hearing a young composer's symphony, which had not received the expected and commensurate acclaim, Schumann writes:

It can move me, when an artist whose course of education can be called neither unsound nor unnatural, . . . [who spent] sleepless nights, which he gave to the piece, working, destroying, again constructing, again despairing (perhaps interrupted here and there by a moment of genius), now receives nothing from the audience, nothing short of nothing, not even the recognition of avoided mistakes. . . . How he stood there, so tense, restless, sad, hoping for a voice which would give him quiet applause! It can move me.[130]

In estimating any young composer's merits, Schumann asks the listener to consider the composer's training, and to keep in mind the composer's development.

Love him, . . . but do not forget that only through years of study has

51

he attained poetic freedom, and respect his never resting moral strength. Do not look for the abnormal in him, go back to the basis of his creation; do not measure his genius by his latest symphony, whatever bold and immense [idea] it may express.[131]

In spite of Schumann's sympathetic attitude to young composers, he asks them to recognize the limitations of their ability.

We wish to advice all of those who, although not blessed with genius, happen to be composing, and who want to employ their zeal for the good of art, to continue working diligently; but with the request that they do not have everything published. . . . One should keep his first attempts within his four happy walls.[132]

Furthermore, he never judges the experienced and the inexperienced by the same standard.

The composer seems young. . . . Who will want to judge him according to the same standard by which one judges masters? But if he continues as he has begun, if also he develops step by step toward an independent style, then we may expect [something] really pleasing from him.[133]

Schumann's justice is shown also in his criticism of more accomplished composers such as Berlioz. Schumann points out that his criticism of the *Symphonie Fantastique* is not based on a full orchestral score.

From the beginning I notice that I can judge only according to the piano reduction, in which, however, the instruments are indicated at the most decisive points.[134]

In judging a mature work, Schumann remains fair by not making a final judgment after only the first hearing. For example, Schumann was disappointed at first with *Tannhäuser*, but after he saw it on the stage he reversed his opinion, and in a letter to his teacher, Heinrich Dorn, January 7, 1846, he advises Dorn to attend a performance of Wagner's work.

I hope you will see *Tannhäuser* by Wagner. It contains [something] deep and original; in general, a hundred times better than his earlier operas, but it also contains many a musical triviality. In conclusion, he can become very important for the stage; and as I know him, he also has the courage for it. I find the technical details, the orchestration excellent, without comparison more masterful than before. He already has gone on to complete a new text, *Lohengrin*.[135]

In his criticisms of established composers, Schumann requires high standards. Many times he seems harsh, and appears to lack compassion, but he is usually correct in his estimates. Although

Giacomo Meyerbeer, for example, was highly praised by his contemporaries, Schumann is undaunted in criticizing his work *Les Huguenots*.

I despise this Meyerbeerian fame from the bottom of my heart; his "Huguenots" are the complete list of all deficiencies and of some few good qualities of his time.[136]

Affection and tolerance for the musical ideas and poetic content of contemporary pieces is displayed often by Schumann. With warm enthusiasm he rejoices over the diligent accomplishment of contemporary artists and encourages talents, for example, Mendelssohn, Chopin and Brahms.

However, Schumann is acutely searching in his appraisal of the general level of nineteenth century music; for it was paradoxical how relatively low the standards of taste had sunk, when simultaneously so many musical geniuses were maturing.

After Beethoven's death an unmistakable superficiality in musical production occurred. Beethoven's influence was recognizable only in a few higher striving musicians, while most of them had lost themselves in an empty floweriness. Especially at the piano, brilliance and Italian sentimentality was in vogue.[137]

The following commentary on the state of music in Germany typifies Schumann's attitude toward Italian operatic composers, for example, Rossini, and German virtuoso composers for the piano, Herz and Hünten.

One cannot say that the musical conditions at that time in Germany were very pleasant. On the stage Rossini was still reigning; at the piano almost completely Herz and Hünten. Yet only a few years had passed since Beethoven, C. M. v. Weber, and Franz Schubert lived among us. To be sure Mendelssohn's star was rising, and wonderful things were heard about a Pole, Chopin—but these had a more permanent effect only later.[138]

In his appraisals of nineteenth century music, Schumann is ready to recognize the existence of great talents, for example, Schubert, Berlioz, and Brahms. However, as has been shown earlier in this chapter, Schumann is a composer first and a critic second. An examination of his music reveals the principles underlying his criticism of the works of others. As a musician, Schumann is never a revolutionary who rejects the past and as a substitute attempts to create something shockingly novel, but rather he is a synthesist who strives for a unification of two worlds. This attitude is typical of the romantic, who looks to ancient and medieval civilization, as well as to the contemporary, for inspiration. Although after 1840 Schumann concentrates more on baroque and classic models, he does employ styles and forms from a past era in his compositions written between 1830-1840. For instance, Schumann writes a chorale-like section at the end of the piece "Ende vom Lied" (Example 6, p. 55). Often he composes pieces which are folk-like in character, as found in the waltz-like section at the end of the *Davidsbündlertänze* (Example 7, p. 56). Furthermore, in his piano compositions Schumann incorporates genuine folk music, which has an anonymous origin, and "composed" folk music, which has a known author.[139] Thus, Schumann is able to evoke the music of a previous era while still imbuing the work with his own romantic temper.

Schubert was one of the nineteenth century composers whom Schumann most revered and promoted. As a composer Schumann acknowledges a great debt to Schubert. He praises Schubert's technical skill, but even more his ability to capture the essence of life itself in music.

Here is, besides masterly musical technique of composition, in addition, life in all its facets, coloration into finest nuances, meaning everywhere, the sharpest expression of the single elements, and finally poured out over the whole a romanticism which is known elsewhere in Franz Schubert. And this heavenly length of the symphony [is] like a thick four volume novel, let us say, by Jean Paul, who also cannot come to an end, to be sure for best of reasons, in order to allow the reader to recreate it afterwards.[140]

Berlioz, who has a special appeal for Schumann, because Schumann sees him as attempting to unite literary and musical ideas, is heralded as one of the progressive spirits of the age. Although, when Schumann was writing this criticism, he thought Berlioz to be ten years younger than he was, he accepted him as an accomplished composer.

Such a musical man, scarcely nineteen years old [*sic*], of French blood, superabounding in strength, moreover struggling with the future and perhaps with other vigorous passions, is seized for the first time by the God of Love.[141]

The acknowledgment of Brahms' genius is to Schumann's credit. In 1853 when, at the age of twenty, Brahms came to Düsseldorf, he was acclaimed as a genius by Schumann in the article "Neue Bahnen"; further evidence of Schumann's esteem for Brahms appears in a letter to Joseph Joachim dated March 10, 1885.

Example Number 6. Robert Schumann, <u>Phantasiestücke,</u>
Opus 12, "Ende vom Lied", Volume 2, p. <u>121.</u>

Example Number 7. Robert Schumann, Davidsbündlertänze, Opus 6, Number 18 (First edition), Volume 1, p. 131.

The first sonata [*Opus 1*] as the first published work, was a work as has never appeared before, and all four movements form a unit. Thus, one delves deeper and deeper into the other works, as into the *Balladen* [*Opus 10*], the like of which have never before existed. If only he, like you, Sir, would write in larger forms, for orchestra and chorus, that would be marvelous.[142]

Schumann possesses an outstanding ability to recognize geniuses, although a few of his swans turn out to be geese. For example Schumann praises the pianist-composer Moscheles highly, as seen in the following quotation, although the latter never achieved the important place as a composer in the history of music which Schumann expected of him.

In Moscheles we have the rarer example of a musician who, although older in years and still occupied unceasingly with the study of old masters, observes also the course of more recent phenomena and has made use of their progress. How he now controls those influences with his innate individuality! Thus out of such a mixture of old, new, and [that which is his] own, arises a work such as the latest concerto, clear and sharp in its forms, approaching the romantic in character, yet original, as one knows the composer.[143]

Schumann not only champions the cause of romanticism, but he also believes that German musicians should be more conscious of their tradition. The yearning for consciousness of a national spirit, which is a predominant trait in the romantic period, plays an important role in rejuvenating an interest for the whole German tradition. Schumann hopes German composers will utilize their tradition and not perpetually imitate the Italian.

We believe that the German artistic element today still prevails in the composer; but significant progress begins only with the decisive rejection of all dilettantish pleasure, all Italian influences. Don't we Germans have our own way of singing? Have not the last years proven that there are still minds and masters in Germany who know how to associate profundity with lightness, significance with grace? Spohr, Mendelssohn and others—don't they know how to sing, or to write for singers? . . . The highest peaks of Italian art do not even reach the first beginnings of genuine German art. One cannot stand with one foot on an Alp and with the other in a comfortable meadow.[144]

He vehemently criticizes contemporary Italian composers, and because one of their more obvious faults is a lack of musical content, he compares them to butterflies. "See the fluttering lovely butterfly, but take away the colorful scales, and see how pitifully he flits about, and how little attention he is given." [145]

Schumann also criticizes the Italian preoccupation with melodies, and distinguishes between the creative gift for composing melody and the minor talent for making up tunes.

. . . not everything which is easily singable is melody; there is a difference between melody and melodies. Whoever has melody, will have melodies; who, however, has melodies, will not always have the former; the child sings his melodies to himself, melody, however, develops only later. In the first two chords of the *Eroica Symphony*, for instance, there lies more melody than in ten Bellini melodies. This, of course, cannot be explained to musical ultramontanists.[146]

His third criticism levelled against the Italians is that they can compose only in one genre, while the Germans are capable of expression in diverse forms.

And exactly this distinguishes the masters of the German school from Italians and Frenchmen, it has made them great and thoroughly educated, that they experimented in all forms and genre, whereas the masters of those other nations distinguished themselves only in one genre.[147]

A fourth misgiving he has with the Italian school lies in its superficiality. The music of the Italian school is too theatrical for Schumann.

Rossini is the most excellent scene painter; but take away from him the artificial illumination and the tempting distance of the theater, and see what remains! [148]

Schumann does not criticize Italians merely because they are born on the other side of the Alps, as noted in his overwhelming praise of Palestrina. He writes to Franz Brendel, on July 3, 1848:

Besides, I owe you many thanks for the music you sent me, especially Palestrina. It sometimes sounds like music of the spheres—and at the same time, what art! I, in addition, believe that he is the greatest musical genius whom Italy has produced.[149]

Schumann established two organizations for the realization of his musical ideas and criticisms, the *Davidsbund*, a semifictitious society of artists, and the *Neue Zeitschrift für Musik*, a musical journal. Although the *Davidsbund* is an imaginary, half-humorous, half-poetical fiction of Schumann, it exists in a looser sense in his group of friends who gathered at the *Kaffeebaum*. The society itself is an ideal, more than a reality. But why does Schumann choose the name *Davidsbund?* The musical connection is derived from David, who played the harp; and because he fought against the Philistines, he was associated with opposition to the *status quo*. In the college slang of nineteenth-century Germany, a

"Philistine" is a non-student, who is satisfied to live according to the routine of everyday life, a man of narrow, sober, and prosaic views, as contrasted with a man of poetry.

Members of the society are friends and acquaintances of Schumann, most of whom are all given fictitious names; he includes only people who agree with his ideals. He quietly introduces the principal co-operators in the *Zeitschrift*, and even the composer Berlioz, with whom Schumann was not personally acquainted at the time. Schumann plays a large role in the society, and appears under the names of Florestan, Eusebius, and Raro. Ludwig Schunke, a pianist and composer, is Jonathan; Fritz Friedrich, the painter and music lover, is probably Lyser; Carl Banck, a clever song composer and ardent worker for the society, is Serpentin; Anton von Zuccalmaglio, an arranger of German folksongs and a significant contributor to the *Zeitschrift* is Gottschalk Wedel; Clara appears as Chiara or Zilia (a shortening of Cecilia, who was the patron saint of music), and Felix Mendelssohn is called Felix Meritis. These characters appear in his criticisms, essays, and various writings. Schumann describes himself and other members of the society in the following words: "Florestan and Eusebius is my double nature, which I should like to fuse into a man like Raro. . . . The other disguised ones are to a certain extent living people." [150] Raro plays the role of moderator in discussions between Florestan and Eusebius, which has led scholars to think he might at times have represented Friedrich Wieck, Clara's father.

The organization is essentially a clever device for Schumann to carry on debates and express his views. Schumann states its purpose in an address given at the seventh annual meeting of the *Davidsbund*, in 1841.

With this new annual ring, which our tree has brought forth, I want to recommend to you its further cultivation. The name *Davidsbund* should neither be a vain, nor a fortuitous one. That David slew many a Philistine, may have well occurred to many, when they heard of you. But above all this name should remind us of the eternal, sacred union of poetry and music. The name of the crowned singer, who immortalized himself in divinely inspired songs, shall always point out to us the relationship between art and religion; it shall remind us that the language of a spiritual world may not be deprecated in order to flatter the baser side of man and to gild and embroider the objectionable.

Music should not be handled as a matter of fashion nor like a quickly passing tickle of the senses, which today disguises itself in one form, tomorrow in another. It should not be viewed as a drawing room, where the critics play host, pleasing all. Therefore, I would like to inspire the bearers of the name, the members of the society [*Bündler*], I would like, if I, the weak speaker of this festive occasion, had sufficient power and did not have to guard myself from spinning the thread too long and becoming a victim of my own penal code, I would like to move you to become closer to one another and to lock hands for one purpose, for one goal. Everyone who is given a voice may raise it according to his insight, when judging achievements as well as when speaking about things to be accomplished. We do not intend to honor a famous man nor burn incense before a work which has become part of the daily agenda, but to promote art, to take care of its holy temple here, and to expel by whipping a bunch of salesmen and money changers.

Wherever I cast my eyes I see golden calves on splendid pedestals, and a dancing and billowing crowd around the animal. In so many sacred places I see holy books full of lofty runes, sunken under debris, covered with dust and forgotten, and above them the piled up ballast of feeble, limpid products of poor craftsmanship. Here every member of the organization should not destroy his code of laws, but rather let them be illuminated with a flaming script, so that the eyes of the people are opened, that they may see the calf as calf, so that the old prophets (for singers and seers have all along been designated by the same word) would be brought back to life. But my last final sentence is not a summons to arms against the new; I will not onesidedly overemphasize the old and place it above everything of the future. To recognize all worthy endeavors shall be our motto, to appreciate every merit should be our striving, since something noble and beautiful can mature in every latitude and at every time.[151]

The organ for the realization of the principles of the *Davidsbund* is the *Neue Zeitschrift für Musik*, which Schumann and his colleagues founded in 1834. When Schumann and his friends gathered at the *Kaffeebaum*, he was usually the silent partner, preferring to express himself later, in writing rather than in speech. During the winter of 1833-1834, at one of these meetings, the idea of initiating a new musical journal was proposed; it was a typical protest of youth, feeling itself impelled to originality in art, and in striking forth against existing conditions.

Under these circumstances the battle could have been waged more successfully through works of art rather than by a periodical, but musical criticism also had fallen into decay. The periodical *Cecilia*, which was published by Schott and had been in existence since 1824, was no longer fit for the educated reader, because of the low level of its content. Heinrich Rellstab, one of the leading critics and opponents of Schumann, was associated with two journals, neither of which was particularly good. He was connected with the *Berliner Allgemeine Musikalische Zeitung*, which came to an end in 1830; whereupon he founded his own magazine, *Iris im Gebiet der Tonkunst*, which survived until 1842, and contained many attacks on Schumann. The only periodical of any influence in 1833 was the *Allgemeine Musikalische Zeitung*, which was published in Leipzig by Breitkopf und Härtel; unfortunately it had a narrow outlook, an inane mildness of judgment, and above all a lenity towards the reigning insipidity and superficiality. It provoked Schumann, who had high ideals, so much that he used to call its reviews "honey-painting" [*Honigpinselei*].

On the twenty-first of March, 1834, an advertisement appeared in *Unser Planet* announcing the future publication of the *Zeitschrift*. It read: "Music. Information about a new musical journal with its prospectus". (*Die Musik. Hinweisung auf eine neue musikalische Zeitschrift mit deren Prospekt*).[152] In the small leaflet Schumann criticizes the existing musical journals.

What are the few musical journals which have come into existence so far? Nothing but exercise-grounds for ossified systems, out of which even the best will cannot squeeze a drop of life; nothing but relics of obsolete doctrines which one always purely and simply denies veneration; nothing but partiality and inflexibility which one sorrowfully passes over. Moreover, they are a conglomeration of exaggerated individual ideas, prejudices, unfruitful personal bickerings, and party squabbles which disgust the better young artists.[153]

Schumann goes on to describe the qualifications and viewpoints of the founders. Along with Schumann, the editors at the start were Friedrich Wieck, Ludwig Schunke, and Julius Knorr.

All the active participants in the new magazine are endowed with that poetic ability and intellectual and ethical education, which alone make possible distinction in the field of music. All are above school and party spirit, and have risen to theoretical and practical independence. Their judgments will, therefore, be unbiased, free from any prejudices, and will be given only in the interest of art. They all glow with that enthusiasm without which nothing important and great was ever accomplished. All have finally recognized their profession, and have sufficiently considered their goal for which they . . . want to strive. They will admit only compatriots of mind and spirit to their organization and permit them to strive for their goals.[154]

The idea of raising the level of musical criticism, partly in order to try their strength, must have been attractive to these young artists, since most of them were gifted with the pen and had the advantage of a sound scholarly education. They were all astute in realizing that they were not yet capable of steering the average taste into new waters through their musical creations. This attitude is found in the first number of the *Zeitschrift*, which appeared April 3, 1834, with a German translation of some lines from the prologue to Shakespeare's *Henry VIII:*

> Only they
> That come to hear a merry bawdy play,
> A noise of targets, or to see a fellow
> In a long motley coat guarded with yellow,
> Will be deceived;[155] (Example 8, p. 63).

This passage was appropriate because it expressed the intention of the *Davidsbündler* to contend against a flattering style of criticism, and of seeking to uphold the dignity of art. Moreover, the *Zeitschrift* was to encourage the advent of a new poetic age by recognizing the efforts of young artists.

Schumann believes that it is important for the artist to have a means by which he can explain his own compositions and pertinent experiences concerning them. This sentiment is expressed in the statement of purpose which appeared in the first issue, 1834.

It seemed necessary to provide him [the artist] with an organ, a public place in which he can put down the best of what he has seen with his own eyes, and experienced in his own spirit. Precisely a journal, in which he can protect himself against biased and untrue criticism.[156]

Of the original editors, Schunke was solely a musician, lacking any skill at prose, whereas the other three editors, Schumann, Wieck and Knorr, wrote well. Hartmann of Leipzig was the first publisher and proprietor of the journal; but early in 1835, it passed into the hands of J. A. Barth of Leipzig, shortly after which Schumann became proprietor and sole editor. He retained this position until Franz Brendel took over in 1844, and the only significant contribution Schumann made thereafter was his article on Brahms.

Schumann uses the *Zeitschrift* as a tool in paving the road for a new artistic era, in pointing up current trends, and also in criticizing the existing old-fashioned ones in order to discard them. The critic must have foresight and be able to predict what will endure. "A Journal should not merely mirror the present. The critics must anticipate what is waning and fight it back, as it

Neue Leipziger
Zeitschrift für Musik.

Herausgegeben
durch einen Verein von Künstlern und Kunstfreunden.

> Die allein,
> Die nur ein luſtig Spiel, Geräuſch der Zärtſchen
> Zu hören kommen, oder einen Mann
> Im bunten Rock, mit Gelb verbrämt, zu ſehen,
> Die irren ſich.   Shakſpeare.

Dieſe Zeitſchrift liefert:

Theoretiſche und hiſtoriſche Aufſätze; kunſtäſthetiſche, grammatiſche, pädagogiſche, biographiſche, akuſtiſche u. a. Nekrologe, Beiträge zur Bildungsgeſchichte berühmter Künſtler, Berichte über neue Erfindungen oder Verbeſſerungen, Beurtheilungen ausgezeichneter Virtuoſenleiſtungen, Operndarſtellungen; unter der Aufſchrift: Zeitgenoſſen, Stizzen mehr oder weniger berühmter Künſtler, unter der Rubrik: Journalſchau, Nachrichten über das Wirken anderer kritiſchen Blätter, Bemerkungen über Recenſionen in ihnen, Zuſammenſtellung verſchiedener Beurtheilungen über dieſelbe Sache, eigne Reſultate darüber, auch Antikritiken der Künſtler ſelbſt, ſodann Auszüge aus ausländiſchen, Intereſſantes aus älteren muſikaliſchen Zeitungen.

Belletriſtiſches, kürzere muſikaliſche Erzählungen, Phantaſieſtücke, Scenen aus dem Leben, Humoriſtiſches, Gedichte, die ſich vorzugsweiſe zur Compoſition eignen.

Kritiken über Geiſteserzeugniſſe der Gegenwart mit vorzüglicher Berückſichtigung der Compoſitionen für das Pianoforte. Auf frühere ſchätzbare, übergangene oder vergeſſene Werke wird aufmerkſam gemacht, wie auch auf eingeſandte Manuſcripte talentvoller unbekannter Compeniſten, die Aufmunterung verdienen. Zu derſelben Gattung gehörige Compoſitionen werden öfter zuſammengeſtellt, gegen einander verglichen, beſonders intereſſante doppelt beurtheilt. Zur Beurtheilung eingeſandte Werke werden durch eine vorläufige Anzeige bekannt gemacht; doch beſtimmt nicht das Alter der Einſendung die frühere Beſprechung, ſondern die Vorzüglichkeit der Leiſtung.

Miſcellen, kurzes Muſikbezügliches, Anekdotiſches, Kunſtbemerkungen, literariſche Notizen, Muſikaliſches aus Goethe, Jean Paul, Heinſe, Hoffmann, Novalis, Rochlitz u. A. m.

Correſpondenzartikel nur dann, wenn ſie eigentlichſtes Muſikleben abſchildern. Wir ſtehen in Verbindung mit Paris, London, Wien, Berlin, Petersburg, Neapel, Frankfurt, Hamburg, Riga, München, Dresden, Stuttgart, Caſſel u. a. — Referirende Artikel fallen in die folgende Abtheilung.

Chronik, Muſikaufführungen, Concertanzeigen, Reiſen, Aufenthalt der Künſtler, Beförderungen, Vorfälle im Leben. Es wird keine Mühe geſchenet, dieſe Chronik vollſtändig zu machen, um die Namen der Künſtler ſo oft, wie möglich, in Erinnerung zu bringen.

Noch machen wir vorläufig bekannt, daß, wenn ſich die Zeitſchrift bald einer allgemeinen Theilnahme erfreuen ſollte, der Verleger ſich erboten hat, einen Preis auf die beſte eingeſandte Compoſition, für's erſte auf die vorzüglichſte Pianoforteſonate, zu ſetzen, worüber das Nähere ſeiner Zeit berichtet wird.

Ueber die Stellung, die dieſe neue Zeitſchrift unter den ſchon erſcheinenden einzunehmen gedenkt, werden ſich dieſe erſten Blätter thatſächlich am deutlichſten ausſprechen.

Wer den Künſtler erforſchen will, beſuche ihn in ſeiner Werkſtatt. Es ſchien nothwendig, auch ihm ein Organ zu verſchaffen, das ihn anrege, außer durch ſeinen directen Einfluß, noch durch Wort und Schrift zu wirken, einen öffentlichen Ort, in dem er das Beſte von dem, was er ſelbſt geſehen im eigenen Auge, ſelbſt erfahren im eigenen Geiſt, niederlegen, eben eine Zeitſchrift, in der er ſich gegen einſeitige oder unwahre Kritik vertheidigen könne, ſo weit ſich das mit Gerechtigkeit und Unparteilichkeit überhaupt verträgt.

were, from the future." [157] Furthermore, he uses the *Zeitschrift* as a vehicle to encourage new talent. "Mainly we hope to aid young talented composers, whose road to recognition is usually so greatly obstructed." [158]

Although it might be said that Schumann may have wasted his time criticizing when he should have spent more time composing, it must be remembered that as a romantic he would strive to articulate his ideas both verbally and musically. Through the *Davidsbund* and the *Neue Zeitschrift für Musik*, Schumann is able to fight, with the aid of his friends, against the Philistines, who attempt to prostitute art. If he did not realize the beneficial effect his journalistic career had on his musical development, he would not have clung to it with such affection and persistence, writing month after month. Schumann can be regarded as one of the great music critics.

As editor and music critic, he was able to encourage musical talents and to facilitate an understanding between them and the public. That some of those he praised failed to stand the test of time, is of little significance in comparison to the sincerity, honesty, and generosity with which he greeted new works and composers. He had an innate contempt for facile criticism which lauded everything, regardless of its intrinsic worth. In his criticism he is able to synthesize the aesthetic and technical aspects of music.

CHAPTER V

SCHUMANN'S IDEAS ON COMPOSITION

Schumann believes that writing music begins with inspiration. The composer does not conceive of ideas by outlining a plan; rather he ". . . gives to airy nothing/ A local habitation and a name." [159]

Philosophers imagine the matter to be very much worse than it is; certainly they are mistaken if they think that a composer, who works out an idea, sits down like a preacher on Saturday afternoon and outlines his theme according to the customary three parts and really works it out formally; . . . The musician's [mode of] creation is completely different; and when an image, an idea floats before him, only then indeed will he feel happy in his work, if it comes to him in beautiful melodies, carried by the same invisible hands, as the "golden pails" about which Goethe speaks somewhere.[160, 161]

Although the artist must possess imagination [Geist], he must steadily aim at accomplishing his ideals; furthermore, he should work hard to achieve new arrangements of tones which will enliven the composition, by relying on his experience and technical skill.

Imagination [Geist] is essential, and to show it one must not be lazy. If once [the composer] is engaged in work, he must consider what he has before him; he should not fail to make use of the colorful array of instruments, and must drive like a storm as much through the timpanist as through the violinist. To discover new tone colors for the orchestra [Tonbühne] may be difficult, no matter how necessary they will be to us in discharging all of their whirl of thoughts. But [the composer] can make improvements, as it were, if he notices that every instrument, when stretched beyond its limit, ridden beyond its path, appears again fresh as something new; it can be considered as a new discovery, which many a weak mind, shaking his head when looking in one of our scores . . . hardly can digest.[162]

Improvisation is one of the most natural means for the composer to manifest the idea that comes through inspiration. The marks of improvisation are frequent in Schumann's compositions. His harmony seems more to be formed from the movement of the fingers along the keyboard, than to emanate from the premeditated logic which produces more strict part writing. For Schumann both elements are necessary, the improvisatory and the calculated, the impetuous and the studied; but the former is a prior consideration, because it provides the seed for the composition's development and construction. Schumann notes the sterility of "strict composition", i.e., the work of a student who complies with strict forms set up by his teacher, and praises a "law of measure" which permits phrases to be free from the restraint of barlines.

In free fantasy, the highest unites in music, which we certainly miss in pieces of strict composition—the law of measure with alternating lyrical free meters. Poetry did it in Jean Paul's polymeters and in the old choruses: unrestraint is always more ingenious and spirited than restraint.[163]

Schumann advises young composers to write by starting with emotion. Mainly he wants them to present a musical feeling or sentiment [*Empfindung*].

A composition which does not offer anything to the emotion or offends the feeling, is and remains, at most, nothing more than an exercise even though friends of the neckbreaking [piece] may rejoice greatly.[164]

Because Schumann believes composers should trust their emotions and recognize the first conception as the best, he desires that they express their innermost feelings. "Only what comes from the heart, only what is inwardly created and sung has permanence and outlives time." [165]

Despite the fact that Schumann relies on a first impression, he often complains to Clara about the difficulty of writing music.

All last week was spent composing, but there is no real pleasure in my thoughts and no beautiful melancholy. I already told you about the concerto, it is a hybrid between symphonic-concerto and big sonata; I see I cannot write a concerto for the virtuoso; I must think of something else.[166]

Although he admits the validity of two versions of a composition, he contends that the first version is more valuable.

Two different readings of the same work are often equally good. (*Eusebius.*)

The original one is generally the better. (*Raro.*) [167]

Schumann contends that too many young talents strive to achieve difficult results when, in reality, if they would concentrate on the beauty of its essence, their work would be more successful. No matter how adorned a piece is, it must have a solid structure.

To get to the core of a composition, it should be divested first of all its adornments. Only then will it become apparent whether it is really beautifully formed; only then it will become clear what its essence [*Natur*] is and what art added. And if still a beautiful melody remains, if it also embodies a healthy, noble harmony, then the composer has won and deserves our applause. This requirement seems so simple, yet how seldom is it successfully fullfilled! [168]

As a romantic, Schumann places great importance on the inner mood of the composer. He counsels the artist to be in the proper mental and spiritual condition, an idea which he stresses in a letter to Clara dated March, 1838.

It is not surprising to me that you cannot compose now, since there may be so many people coming in and out of your house. To create and to do so successfully, requires happiness and profound solitude.[169]

Schumann also recognizes that the composer's inspiration depends on the will of the gods. "What we have learned, what we know, no one can take from us. But if we are to work with joy, with happiness, the good gods must lend their assistance." [170]

The opposite of emotion and inspiration is the impersonal, which may take the form of virtuosity. In warning against overemphasis on virtuosity, Schumann does not attack virtuosity itself, but rather its misuse. In a review of Edward Röckel's work Schumann writes:

The composer appears to be a virtuoso of a better order [*Richtung*], that is to say he has not disregarded the soul of the instrument for the brilliance of the mechanics; he considers not only the fingers, but also the heart.[171]

Schumann himself employs virtuostic effects without losing sight of musical value. For example, on the last page of the second movement of the *Phantasie*, Schumann writes extraordinarily wide leaps and still is able to express the musical line (Example 9, p. 68).

According to Schumann's standards, virtuosity does not exclude musicality.

Certainly the young composers always grasped easily enough that music does not exist for the fingers' sake, but vice versa, and that in order to become a good virtuoso one cannot afford to be a poor musician.[172]

Example Number 9. Robert Schumann, _Phantasie,_
Second Movement, Volume 3, p. 111.

Schumann is not opposed to virtuosity *per se*. When it is allied with artistry, he has high praise for it. He lauds the work of Liszt and Thalberg, who do not misuse their technical ability:

No one can deny the former ingenuity regarding technical difficulties, invention of truly new instrumental effects, etc., as little as the latter a drawing-room gracefulness, a calculation and knowledge of the effect, etc., so that everywhere he will captivate and excite.[173]

Schumann, although he envies Liszt's ability as a performing artist, writes to Clara: "Art, as you practice it, and as I often do when composing at the piano, this wonderful geniality [*Gemütlichkeit*], I will not give up for all his brilliance." [174]

According to Schumann, a composer must avoid the impersonal and superficial, working out his ideas in a wholly personal form. The greatest satisfaction a composer can have is to know that he has created something that is totally his own. Schumann expresses this sentiment in one of the *Jugendbriefe*, dated August 8, 1831.

It is such a beautiful thing for a young poet and completely so for a young composer, [that] you can hardly believe what a sensation it is if he can say to himself: this work is completely yours, no one brings this possession to you and no one can take it away from you, for it is wholly yours; oh, understand this "wholly"! Since the reason for this feeling comes but seldom, since genius is only a [fleeting] moment, this feeling breaks forth in its entire beauty and produces a type of calming self-confidence which does not need to fear a faultfinder.[175]

In the development of a composer's personal talent, time plays a major role. However, the development of an artist does not always continue in a straight line, and the composer must be prepared to experience moments when he feels himself retreating rather than progressing.

In order to unearth something great, of quiet beauty, grains of sand must be stolen from [the hourglass of] time; the whole, complete work does not come all at once; much less does it snow down from heaven. That now and then moments come in which one believes oneself regressing, although this last is often only a more or less vacillating progress, lies in nature.[176]

Schumann thinks that an artist should put aside for a while, even for years, an especially difficult composition, returning to it later for final revision. Schumann does not explain the maturing process, but he recognizes the occurrence of this phenomenon in connection with a series of ballads he wrote for voice and piano.

This morning I put in order the first volume of the ballads: *Schatz-gräber*, *Frühlingsfahrt*, and *Abends am Strand*. It gave me pleasure again, because they are three good pieces. There is certainly [something] good in sleeping on a composition, sometimes for a few years.[177]

In Schumann's opinion a composer must develop slowly; and he must not take his first works too seriously, although the composer's early compositions are necessary as building blocks which enable him to produce more mature works. Schumann has a strong, sentimental attachment to his early compositions, for he recognizes their value in the development of his art. He writes to his friend Carl Koszmaly in May, 1843:

With some timidity I enclose a parcel of my old compositions. You will easily perceive how immature and incomplete they are. They are mostly reflections of my agitated youth, the man and musician in me strove for simultaneous expression. It is so, even now that I have learned to command my music and myself better. How much joy and sorrow are buried in this little pile of notes! [178]

The composer who works out an idea, which came to him through inspiration, is formed by many influences, musical and extramusical. He absorbs into music the whole of his experience. Schumann emphasizes the importance of these influences on the artist. According to Hermann Ludwig, Freiherr von der Pfordten, a modern biographer of Schumann: "The deeper the experience, the higher the musical value"; and with this statement as a premise, Pfordten concludes, "the richer the life, the more mature the art".[179]

Schumann uses a number of musical sources in working out his ideas. For example, there is a strong folk-like element in Schumann's music. The "Grossvatertanz", a folk song, appears in the last number of both *Papillons* and *Carnaval* (Examples 10, p. 71 and 11, p. 72). This German folk song was played often as the concluding piece at a dance, and it is placed appropriately at the end of *Papillons*, which portrays a masked ball, and at the conclusion of *Carnaval*, which presents the dancing atmosphere of carnival season. It is interesting to see here how Schumann assimilates folk material into his compositions. In *Papillons* the "Grossvatertanz" is presented first by itself and later in conjunction with a counter melody; the latter is done also in *Carnaval*, where the tune is labeled "Thême du XVIIème Siècle". The tune is transferred then to the treble and modified rhythmically.

Furthermore, Schumann employs songs which, although they

70

Example Number 10. Robert Schumann, <u>Papillons</u>, Opus 2, Number 12, Volume 1, p. 22.

*) Hier muß die Oberstimme glanzvoll schmetternd dominieren, während in dem darauffolgenden Ritornell sanfter Oboenklang vorherrschen soll.

Here the upper part must dominate with a brilliant ringing tone, while in the following Ritornelle, soft Oboe-like sounds should be the most prominent.

Ici, le chant doit ressortir avec une sonorité éclatante, tandisque, dans la ritournelle, c'est le timbre doux du hautbois qui doit prédominer.

Example Number 11. Robert Schumann, Carnaval, Opus 9,
"Marche des 'Davidsbündler' contre les Philistins",
Volume 2, p. 25.

were composed by a known author, are folk-like in nature, such as Claude Joseph Rouget de Lisle's "Marseillaise", which appears in *Faschingsschwank aus Wien* (Example 12, p. 74). Often Schumann's own themes appear to be folk-like in character, for example, the opening bars of the eleventh number of the *Davidsbündlertänze* (Example 13, p. 75). There are also instances in Schumann's music of possible quotes from folk music which are difficult to identify, as in the last number of *Papillons*. In using folk-like themes, Schumann remains true to all their folk characteristics. In Example 14, p. 76 he writes a triple meter dance followed by a typical *Nachtanz*, here a faster duple meter dance.

In addition to folk music, Schumann utilizes the music of previous composers. However, it should be noted that Schumann believes it useless to imitate the musical style of a bygone age, because that style has meaning only for the epoch in which it was created.

There is a class of sonatas which are most difficult to discuss; they are those correctly written, honest, well-meant sonatas which the Mozart-Haydn school produced by the hundred and of which even today specimens are brought to light here and there. If they are criticized, the common sense of the one who produced them would have to be criticized. They have natural cohesion, well-proportioned structure [*wohlanständige Haltung*]. . . . But certainly to attract attention today, indeed even to please, takes more than simply being honest. . . . In short, the sonata style of 1790 is not that of 1840; the demands as to form and content have risen everywhere.[180]

Men sometimes forget that the past was once the present, an argument Schumann brings forth when people tell him about bygone glories.

How often does man sigh and say, ah, how empty is the present, and how beautiful was the past! But he does not realize that the past at one time must have been the present. Or, [that] the present is like a dream; only after it has passed, do we become conscious of it.[181]

Although a composer must strive to be original, at the same time he must study and honor the scores of previous eras. Schumann bemoans the fact that those who try merely to please the public fancy often limit themselves to contemporary music, and do not study different styles to broaden their vision. For example, Schumann strove to study musical literature of the baroque period. Eugenie Schumann quotes from her father's *Tagebuch*, in which he expresses a desire to learn the older literature.

73

Example Number 12. Robert Schumann, Faschingsschwank aus Wien, Opus 26, "Allegro", Volume 4, p. 134.

Example Number 13. Robert Schumann, Davidsbündlertänze, Opus 6, Number 11 (First edition), Volume 1, p. 121.

Example Number 14. Robert Schumann, Papillons, Opus 2, Number 12, Volume 1, p. 22.

*) Hier muß die Oberstimme glanzvoll schmetternd dominieren, während in dem darauffolgenden Ritornell sanfter Oboenklang vorherrschen soll.

Here the upper part must dominate with a brilliant ringing tone, while in the following Ritornelle, soft Oboe-like sounds should be the most prominent.

Ici, le chant doit ressortir avec une sonorité éclatante, tandisque, dans la ritournelle suivante, c'est le timbre doux du hautbois qui doit prédominer.

For a long time I have had in mind, together with Clara, looking more at older music (before Bach's time). About old Italians and Netherlanders, even Germans, we know but little. And really it is so necessary that an artist be able to account for himself before the whole history of his art.[182]

The works of Beethoven were a substantial influence upon Schumann. For example, the last number of *Carnaval* echoes the spirit of the last movement of Beethoven's *Emperor Concerto*. It is of further interest that Schumann combines his rhythmic treatment of the "Grossvatertanz" with the melody of Beethoven's theme (Examples 15, p. 78 and 16, p. 79). Both Schumann and Beethoven resort to variations on similar bass themes as the foundation for a composition. Beethoven does it in the last movement of the *Eroica Symphony*, and Schumann in the *Impromptus* (Examples 17, p. 80 and 18, p. 81). The second "Impromptu", which is in C major, begins on the dominant seventh chord of F major and moves to C major a few bars later, which is similar to the harmonic movement at the beginning of *Symphony No. 1* by Beethoven (Examples 19, p. 82 and 20, p. 83).

Schumann's response to music is similar to Beethoven's; Schumann is not attempting consciously to imitate Beethoven and may not even realize that a relationship exists. For example, the "Soldatenmarsch" from the *Album für die Jugend*, which was written after 1840, bears so strong a resemblance to the third movement of the *Sonata*, Opus 24 for violin and piano (Examples 21, p. 84 and 22, p. 85), that had he recognized it he might have avoided it as a plagiarism.

The theme of the *Impromptus* is borrowed from Clara, who had a strong musical influence on Schumann. She also gave him a musical motive for the *Davidsbündlertänze* and the theme for the "Quasi Variazioni" of the *Konzert ohne Orchester*. Schumann also borrows from some of his friends and contemporaries. The theme for the *Symphonische Etüden*, Opus 13, is based on a theme by Baron von Fricken, the father of Ernestine; and "Etüde XII" of the *Symphonische Etüden* employs a melody from Marschner's opera *Der Templer und die Jüdin*.

Schumann uses the renaissance and baroque device of a *soggetto cavato* in some of his works, adapting to music letters suggested by the names or locations of some of his friends. The *Variationen über den Namen Abegg* are based on the tones A, B flat, E, G, G, and are dedicated to "Comtesse Pauline von Abegg".[183] The letters in the name of a small Bohemian town,

Example Number 15. Robert Schumann, Carnaval, Opus 9,
"Marche des 'Davidsbündler' contre les Philistins",
Volume 2, p. 25.

Example Number 16. Five Piano Concertos. Ludwig van
Beethoven, "Concerto Number 5", Opus 73, Third
Movement (Rondo-Allegro), p. 162.

Example Number 17. The Nine Symphonies of Beethoven
in Score, "Symphony Number 3", Opus 55, Fourth
Movement (Finale-Allegro molto), pp. 87-88.

Example Number 18. Robert Schumann, <u>Impromptus</u>, Opus 5, Number 1 (First edition), Volume 1, p. 77.

Impromptus
über ein Thema von Clara Wieck

Impromptus
on a theme by Clara Wieck

Impromptus
sur un thème de Clara Wieck

Impromptus
über ein Thema von Clara Wieck

Symphonie N⁰ 1.

I.

L. van Beethoven, Op. 21

Example Number 21. Robert Schumann, Album für die Jugend, Opus 68, "Soldatenmarsch", Volume 5, p. 36.

43 Klavierstücke
Album für die Jugend
43 Piano Pieces   43 Pièces de piano
Album for the young   Album à la jeunesse

Robert Schumann, Op. 68
Komponiert 1848

Melodie   Melody   Mélodie

Soldatenmarsch
Soldiers' March   Marche militaire

84

Asch, which was the home of Ernestine von Fricken, form a musical basis for most of the pieces in *Carnaval*. And the "Nordisches Lied" from the *Album für die Jugend*, dedicated to the Danish composer Niels Gade, is based on the letters of his name.

Another way in which Schumann draws on his musical experiences is by making piano arrangements of other composers' works. Schumann's approach to transcription developed as he matured artistically. As a younger man he favored transliteration, that is, a close rendering of the original text; in 1832 he arranged six of the Paganini caprices for piano. This first set of Paganini caprices, Opus 3, is more nearly a transliteration of Paganini's text. For this reason, the compositions contained in Opus 3 are not as pianistic as those in Opus 10. For example, Schumann copies the middle section of the thirteenth Paganini caprice almost note for note without regard for the resulting awkward, unpianistic leaps (Examples 23, p. 87 and 24, p. 88). However, the second set, Opus 10, contains more originality, and is a transcription rather than a transliteration, giving the impression of having been recomposed for the piano (Examples 25, p. 89 and 26, p. 90).[184]

As an older and more experienced composer, he wrote accompaniments to the six Bach solo violin sonatas and partitas. Although to twentieth-century ears the accompaniments to the Bach violin works may seem questionable, Schumann sincerely believes he is true to Bach's intentions. Furthermore, Bach himself transcribed movements from his solo violin sonatas and partitas. For example, the "Preludio" from *Partita* Number 3 appears as the "Sinfonie" from the Cantata Number 29, "Wir danken dir, Gott", and the "Fuga" from the *Sonata* Number 1 as "Fuga" for organ in D minor (Schmieder Number 539).

Schumann erects an important criterion for evaluating arrangements, namely that the composer remain faithful to the work's original spirit. Concerning Liszt's transcriptions of some of Schubert's songs, Schumann writes:

It boils down to the old question of whether the interpretive artist may place himself above the creative artist; whether the former may change the latter's work arbitrarily. The answer is easy: we laugh at a foolish person, if he does it badly; we allow an intelligent person [*einen Geistreichen*] to do it, provided he does not altogether destroy something of the meaning of the original. In the school of piano playing this type of transcription deserves a special chapter.[185]

Example Number 23. Nicolo Paganini, Capricen für Violine solo, Opus 1, Number 13, p. 26.

Example Number 24. Robert Schumann, Studien für das Pianoforte nach Capricen von Paganini, Opus 3, Number 4, Volume 1, p. 45.

Example Number 25. Nicolo Paganini, <u>Capricen</u> <u>für</u>
Violine solo, Opus 1, Number 6, p. 12.

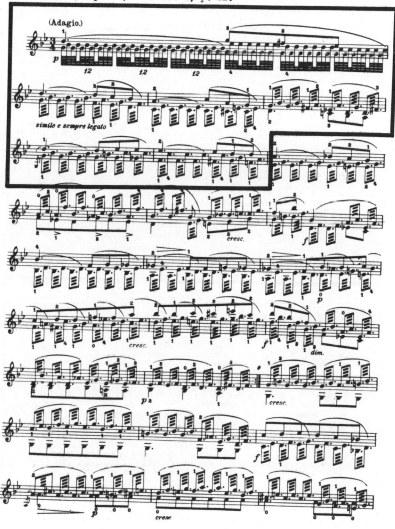

Example Number 26. Robert Schumann, Sechs Konzert-Etüden Komponiert nach Capricen von Paganini, Opus 10, Number 2, Volume 2, p. 34.

In composing, Schumann takes into account all his experiences, using even his own previous work as a source of ideas by transferring motives from one piece to another. In the "Intermezzo" Opus 4, Number 6 Schumann quotes the *soggetto cavato* ABEGG, which is the basis of the *Variationen über den Namen Abegg* (Example 27, p. 92), and in the third of the *Davidsbündlertänze* (1837) Schumann employs a motive from the "Promenade" in *Carnaval* (1835) (Example 28, p. 93). Although other composers had used a similar device, Schumann employs it more programmatically. For instance, a theme from the "Finale" of *Papillons* is used originally to depict the dissolution of a masked ball. But later in *Carnaval*, Schumann takes the same theme and develops it to produce a self-portrait. Here in "Florestan", the theme is first stated, then reinforced with octaves, repeated, inverted, extended, and finally expanded in arpeggio (Examples 29, p. 94 and 30, p. 95).

Cyclic form was not new with Schumann; but he employs it in a new romantic way, as a basis for developing a composition. "It was not satisfactory working an idea out only in one movement; it was concealed in other forms and modifications. . . ." [186] His use of cyclic form, involving the recurrence of motives and themes in multi-movement works, is quite ingenious. The theme used in the first number of *Papillons* also appears in the "Finale", where it is stated, then delayed rhythmically, and finally dissolved. And the measures marked "Presto", which conclude the "Préambule" from *Carnaval*, also come at the end of the "Marche des 'Davidsbündler' contre les Philistins", where they are extended.

Finally, Schumann concentrates on single themes to the extent of writing monothematic pieces. For example, in "Eusebius" from *Carnaval* Schumann repeats the theme with different scorings, and varies it rhythmically by replacing the septuplet with a quintuplet and a triplet (Example 31, p. 96).

In addition to musical influences, extramusical phenomena play a significant role in the total experience behind Schumann's music. Schumann's use of the extramusical may be shown by comparing his sketches with those of Beethoven. The latter also relies on extramusical phenomena: "I always have a picture in my mind when composing, and follow its lines." [187] However, Beethoven does not expect strict programmatic connotations. "The description of a picture belongs to painting. . . . my sphere extends further into other regions." [188] Beethoven, moreover, may

Example Number 27. Robert Schumann, Intermezzi, Opus 4, Number 6, Volume 1, p. 74.

Example Number 28. Robert Schumann, Davidsbündlertänze,
Opus 6, Number 3 (First edition), Volume 1, p. 108.

Papillons

Fräulein Therese, Rosalie und Emilie gewidmet

Example Number 30. Robert Schumann, <u>Carnaval</u>, Opus 9, "Florestan", Volume 2, p. 8.

Eusebius

have had a picture in mind when composing, but he does not reveal it to the listener. Schumann, on the other hand, uses extramusical phenomena somewhat differently. For him a phenomenon stimulates an emotion which he expresses in music. As a guide to the listener he often uses a title which describes the source of inspiration or nature of the emotion being presented.

The following passages indicate the effect extramusical phenomena had on Schumann:

I gave the Dutch maiden a soft sweet kiss, and when I came home about nine o'clock, I sat down at the piano . . . at the piano the thought of the Fandango occurred to me—then I was exceedingly happy. As I stopped, I looked out of the window up to the beautiful spring sky . . . and as I thought about butterflies, a beautiful night butterfly fluttered toward the window. That had a beautiful meaning for me, . . .[189]

As I was composing I continually saw funeral processions, coffins, unhappy, despairing men; and when I was finished with the composition and sought a title for a long time, I kept coming back to this: "Funeral Fantasia"—Isn't that remarkable—As I was composing I also was so moved that tears came to my eyes and I still did not know why.[190]

Schumann's general disposition was colored by such indirect factors as the weather. "Today is a heavenly day in May [June, 1832], thus, I want to create and work, and with diligence and action be thankful to my genius which sustains me." [191]A more direct influence on the musician is the experience he gains by changing environment. If a creative artist, according to Schumann, does not reside in an artistic center, his ability to produce great works may be restricted. But after examining the lives of several prominent composers such as Bach, who lived his whole life in Germany, mostly in smaller provincial cities, Schumann is forced to modify his belief.

Among all artists, trips are the least profitable, certainly, for musicians . . . more for the poet, most profitable for the painter. Our great composers always have dwelt quietly in one and the same place, for example, Bach, Haydn, Beethoven, although a view of the Alps or of Sicily might not have harmed them.[192]

For Schumann, the composer's environment influences his works. Schumann believes that without a climate of progressive ideas, the composer's thoughts will be drowned amid the undertow of conservative currents.

The composer [G. Flügel] lives in a small city, and this is, I believe, the cause for what is lacking: grace, flexibility, and a sense for delicate phrases [*feiner Takt*]. We wish that the future will endow him with these qualities and that he will not be deprived completely of the opportunity to change his sphere of action. Then we will remind the public with pleasure of this young composer, whom we believe we must judge more strictly in proportion to [his] more seriously striving talent.[193]

"Tell me where you live, and I will tell you how you compose." There is some truth in this paradox of Florestan, who even wants the reversed situation to be found correct. Walks, journeys are hardly to the point, even though they exert a momentary influence. But lock Beethoven for ten years in a little corner (the thought is outrageous), and see whether he finished a D minor symphony there.[194]

One of the greatest mistakes composers who live in provincial localities make is to attempt to imitate contemporary fashions without understanding them.

And it is unfortunate, when musical 'Babbitts' [*Kleinstadtbewohner*] suddenly wish to behave in a fashionable Parisian manner; a misfortune which regrettably is more common with us in Germany than anywhere else.[195]

In addition to impersonal factors, people, for example Clara Wieck, exercised a significant influence on Schumann's musical development. From approximately 1835 to 1840 he battled with Herr Wieck over Clara, but concurrently he composed some of his greatest piano music, the *Phantasiestücke*, Opus 12, *Kinderszenen*, and the *Phantasie*, Opus 17. In a letter to Clara dated June 8, 1839, he reveals his dependence upon Clara and the emotional effect of his battle with Herr Wieck.

I have entered today my twenty-ninth year; perhaps the greater half of my life already lies behind me. Anyway I will not become very old, that I certainly know. My great inner passions have raged within me, and grief about you also has gnawed at me. But you, as well, are the one who will again bring peace and healing to me. Today, for instance, I am not sad. How could I be! Heaven has, after all, preserved me from want and blessed me with spiritual strength. My happiness is complete except for domestic order, peace, and security.[196]

He acknowledges his debt to Clara, in a letter to Heinrich Dorn dated September 5, 1839.

Certainly much of the struggle which Clara has cost me may be contained in my music, and surely may have been understood by you. The concerto, the sonata, the *Davidsbündlertänze*, *Kreisleriana*, and the *Novelleten* she, almost alone, brought about.[197]

The concept of yearning for an unattainable ideal was part of Clara's appeal to Schumann, as well as a romantic symptom.

As a part of his total experience, the piano has a crucial function in the development of Schumann's genius. He set out to become a pianist and pursued this interest by studying under Friedrich Wieck. Driven by a passionate desire to achieve a perfect technique as quickly as possible, he devised a contrivance by which the greatest dexterity would be attained. Because of the device he strained the tendons in his fourth finger, crippled it, and for some time injured his whole hand. Fortunately, this serious condition was alleviated by medical treatment; although he recovered enough use of his hand to play the piano, there was no possibility of his becoming a virtuoso. He was confronted with the problem of how to continue developing as a musician, and for the world it was a blessing that he devoted himself to composition.

Although the piano was the first instrument seriously to influence him, he did not compose exclusively for it; even among his youthful works of the 1820s some songs, a symphony and a piano quartet exist. In 1839, almost at the end of his first and most fruitful period of piano composition, he writes:

Piano music forms an important section in the newer history of music. . . . The most significant talents of the present are pianists. . . . The instrument has been . . . perfected to a high degree. With the ever-progressing mechanics of piano playing, with the bolder impetus which composition took through Beethoven, the instrument continued to grow in extensiveness and significance.[198]

Schumann conceives in pianistic terms; in fact, until 1845 he always composed at the piano. "It was only from the year 1845 on, when I began to invent and work out everything in my head, that a completely new type of composing technique began to develop." [199] Schumann is aware of the potential of the piano and the course of development it had taken with his predecessors, as well as the trend it was following.

The older I become, the more I see how the piano, particularly in three aspects, expresses itself essentially and characteristically, through the fullness of voices and flow of harmony (as with Beethoven, Franz Schubert), through the use of the pedal (as with Field), or through rapidity of execution [*Volubilität*] (as with Czerny, Herz). . . . Broadly trained composer-virtuosi, like Hummel, Moscheles and finally Chopin, apply all three means together and therefore are most loved by the players.[200]

99

Schumann likes to experiment with the piano to obtain unusual effects. He is ingenious in choosing pedal markings which will obtain the particular sounds he desires. In the final measures of the introduction to the *Sonata*, Opus 11, Schumann has the pianist hold the pedal through the arpeggiation of an F sharp minor triad to obtain more volume. Then the pedal is lifted on the octave C sharp so that the C sharp may sound out pianissimo. When the chord vanishes, the listener is able to imagine a dominant effect which resolves to a tonic harmony (Example 32, p. 101). In the last four measures of *Papillons* (Example 33, p. 102), Schumann asks the pianist to hold the pedal until after the A of the chord is sounded. Then when the pedal is lifted it enhances the role of the fingers in evaporating the chord. Schumann achieves the opposite effect in the "Finale alla Fantasia" of the *Variationen über den Namen Abegg* where the pedal is put down after the G is played, in order to fill out the *soggetto cavato* by enhancing the sound (Example 34, p. 103).

The pedal directions Schumann writes for the execution of the last chord in "Paganini" from *Carnaval* often are misunderstood (Example 35, p. 104). Although custom has held that when playing the second chord the keys are to be depressed silently, it is valid only for a small room. It is necessary to touch the chord softly when the piece is performed in the concert hall, because not all the notes in the dominant seventh chord on E flat will sound out properly as partials over F and A flat. In the third variation of the second movement of the *Sonata*, Opus 14, the pedal is used to achieve a romantic effect of restrained passion (Example 36, p. 105). If the notes were played without the pedal, they would have a light staccato effect. But by holding the pedal for eight bars, Schumann blurs the harmony, repressing the directness of the music and adding a subtle complexity to the measures.

Schumann's interest in the piano extends to experimentation not only with the pedal, but also with notation. Although Schumann is probably not aware of overtones, which had not been scientifically investigated at the time, he is perhaps conscious of the harmonic divisions of the string.[201] Due to Schumann's interest in ancient philosophy and his desire at one time to collect quotations from Greek and Roman philosophers on music, he may have been acquainted with Pythagoras' work in connection with the monochord.[202] If the small notes in "Promenade" from *Carnaval* are examined, they seem to follow a natural progression

Example Number 32. Robert Schumann, Grosse Sonate, Opus 11, "Introduzione", Volume 2, p. 57.

103

Example Number 35. Robert Schumann, <u>Carnaval</u>, Opus 9,
"Paganini", Volume 2, p. 19.

*) Nur bei genauer Beobachtung der Vorschrift für den Pedalgebrauch wird der beabsichtigte Effe
Only by precise attention to the indications for the use of the pedal will the effect intended be obtained.
On n'obtiendra l'effet prévu qu'en observant exactement les prescriptions relatives à l'emploi de la pédale.

Example Number 36. Robert Schumann, Sonata,
Opus 14, Second Movement, Volume 3, p. 26.

) Der Herausgeber spielt entgegen R. Sch Vorschrift diese Variation ganz ohne Pedal.
Contrary to Robert Schumann's instructions, the editor plays this Variation entirely without pedal
Le réviseur joue cette variation entièrement sans pédale, contrairement aux indications de Schumann

from the first, to the second, to the third, and then to the fourth harmonic division of the string. The fourth division is presented an octave lower than its normal position and just before the third division (Example 37, p. 107).

Schumann's desire to achieve interesting keyboard effects sometimes governs his harmony. Using traditional harmony he is able to achieve new sounds by unusual spacing of chords (Example 38, p. 108). Schumann may be more concerned with the tonal effect produced from a series of chords, than with proper voice leading as seen in Example 39, p. 109, where parallel fifths occur. Furthermore, Schumann is not reluctant to use chords in uncommon positions for the sake of a consistent keyboard structure. In Example 40, p. 110, a diminished chord is used in root position (measure 5, score 1). The chord is part of a downward moving sequence, and in order to keep the chord in the same position as other similar chords in the sequence, Schumann writes it in root position. Schumann sometimes uses the Neapolitan chord in root position, rather than in first inversion, and thus disregards the problem of a tritone movement in the bass, in order to preserve a keyboard succession of downward moving fifths (Example 41, p. 111).

Schumann's interest in sound extends to other matters, such as the selection of appropriate keys. Wolfgang Boetticher in his voluminous study of Schumann has attempted to associate Schumann's moods and emotions according to keys. Most of Boetticher's results are derived from vocal works in which these relationships can be indicated more easily, and he gives only a few examples from Schumann's piano music written between 1830-1840.[203] He relates D major to happiness and youth, as in the *Novelletten*, Numbers 5 and 8; F sharp minor to something magical, but also partially enshrouded in darkness, as in the third number in *Papillons*, and the first of the *Intermezzi;* G sharp minor to tragedy, which has hidden implications, as in "Fast zu ernst" from *Kinderszenen;* and B flat minor to the contrasting feelings of deepest pain as in the first of the *Drei Romanzen*, or of comfort. The other connections he draws on are from *Album für die Jugend*, which have programmatic captions above them, and from *Vier Märsche*, Opus 76, which were written after 1840. It may be possible to transfer the vocal results to his absolute music, which Boetticher attempts, but it is a speculative undertaking. These matters should be related to direct evidence from the

Example Number 37. Robert Schumann, Carnaval, Opus 9,
"Promenade", Volume 2, p. 21.

a & b = 1st harmonic division   d = 4th harmonic division
c = 2nd harmonic division   e = 3rd harmonic division

Example Number 38. Robert Schumann, <u>Sechs</u> Konzert-Etüden <u>Komponiert nach</u> Capricen <u>von</u> Paganini, Opus 10, Number 6, Volume 2, p. 53.

Example Number 39. Robert Schumann, Studien für das Pianoforte nach Capricen von Paganini, Opus 3, Number 2, Volume 1, p. 39.

Example Number 40. Robert Schumann, Studien für das
Pianoforte nach Capricen von Paganini, Opus 3,
Number 2, Volume 1, p. 40.

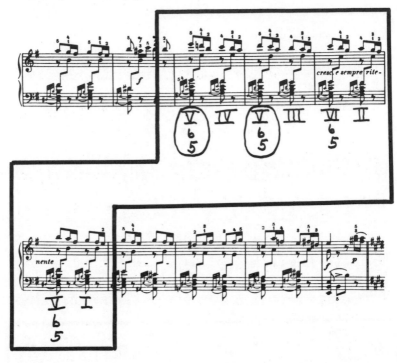

Example Number 41. Robert Schumann, Davidsbündlertänze, Opus 6, Number 17 (First edition), Volume 1, p. 130.

composer himself, that is, where Schumann defines the connection between a definite mood and a key.

Fortunately, two important quotations exist in which Schumann discusses the interconnection between keys and extramusical connotations. In the first he correlates the twelve keys with the months of the year, although he seems to change his mind about including minor keys.

May is the A minor key in nature and dissolves itself luxuriantly in June in C major. Perhaps the twelve keys which exist could be traced back to the twelve months. E major might be August, D major would be July, etc. Of course the minor keys would be missing, but Nature certainly has none, and is eternally young, eternally glorious, and only when the month bids farewell does it appear sad.[204]

Schumann, in his *Damenkonversationslexikon,* a book of aphorisms and definitions, discusses the process by which a composer selects a key.

The true composer comes of his own accord upon the right [key], as the true painter his colors. The difference between major and minor must be admitted indisputably. The former is the active masculine principle, the latter the suffering feminine. Simpler creations have simpler keys; complex [creations] prefer to move around in a foreign region and are, therefore, for keys which the ear has heard less often.[205]

Schumann evokes ideas by harmonic and rhythmic devices, as well as through keys. For example, Schumann creates the feeling of mystic vagueness through harmony. Throughout Schumann's piano music lie countless examples of "romantic harmony", and it is not unusual for him to describe harmony in the following terms: "It is with music as with chess. The queen (melody) has the greatest power, but the king (harmony) always decides the game." [206]

Schumann is able to give the impression of mystic vagueness through cadences which do not end on the tonic chord in root position. In Example 42, p. 113, to avoid a feeling of finality Schumann moves from a dominant chord to a tonic chord in first inversion, rather than in root position. Schumann may not have wanted a decisive cadence here, because it would reinforce A major, the tonality he is trying to avoid. Moreover, this section is in F sharp minor and the use of a strong cadence in A major would destory the feeling for the F sharp minor contrast.

By ending pieces on a chord in second inversion Schumann creates an even greater impression of vagueness. In the fourteenth

Example Number 42. Robert Schumann, Papillons, Opus 2, Number 3, Volume 1, p. 13.

of the *Davidsbündlertänze* (Example 43, p. 115), Schumann concludes on a six-four chord, and there is no pedal direction which would allow the E flat to be sustained until the end of the piece. In "Eusebius" from *Carnaval*, Schumann again concludes on a six-four chord at the midpoint and at the end (Example 44, p. 116). By the same musical technique, he is able to portray the dreamy personality of Eusebius in both pieces.

In "Bittendes Kind", from *Kinderszenen*, Schumann achieves a sense of uncertainty by concluding on a dominant seventh chord, which is resolved to a tonic triad in the next piece (Example 45, p. 117). In another piece from *Kinderszenen*, "Kind im Einschlummern", Schumann goes a step farther in attempting to eradicate a sense of finality, by ending the piece on a subdominant, which first stands in second inversion, rather than a tonic triad (Example 46, p. 118). Although the subdominant ending gives more of a sense of finality than the conclusion of "Bittendes Kind", nevertheless it is not the key of the piece, E minor, nor the tonality to which he is heading. If, however, the next piece, "Der Dichter Spricht", which is in G major, is played immediately, the subdominant triad could be heard as a supertonic triad in G major, followed by dominant and tonic triads (score 3, measure 1).

Schumann also writes deceptive progressions and deceptive cadences to create the impression of mystery. In Example 47, p. 119, he creates an interesting cadential effect. A deceptive progression occurs when the dominant seventh chord in D major is followed by another dominant seventh chord, rather than being resolved. In Example 48, p. 120, Schumann moves from one secondary dominant chord to another in measure 1 of the first score, and in measure 2 he deceptively resolves a dominant seventh chord. Then when the B flat tonic triad appears in measure 3, score 1, and in measures 1 and 2, score 2, it is still not in root position, but rather in second inversion.

Through the use of various other devices Schumann is able to cloud the harmony in order to give the impression of mystic vagueness. In Example 49, p. 121, Schumann not only composes chromatically modulating sequences, but he also employs suspensions, appogiaturas and passing tones. An impression of mystery is further emphasized by the quiet dynamic level and the rapid tempo. These factors are also present in Example 50, p. 122. Here Schumann uses chromatics to modulate quickly from one key to another and employs many non-harmonic tones in an attempt to

Example Number 43. Robert Schumann, Davidsbündlertänze, Opus 6, Number 14 (First edition), Volume 1, p. 125.

Example Number 44. Robert Schumann, Carnaval, Opus 9, "Eusebius", Volume 2, p. 7.

Example Number 46. Robert Schumann, Kinderszenen,
Opus 15, "Kind im Einschlummern", Number 12, Volume 3, p. 57.

Der Dichter spricht

The Poet speaks   Le Poète parle

*)Dieser Doppelschlag ist sehr ruhig auszuführen | This turn should be played very tranquilly | Ce grupetto doit être exécuté très calme

118

Example Number 47. Robert Schumann, Novelletten,
Opus 21, Number 8, Volume 4, p. 81.

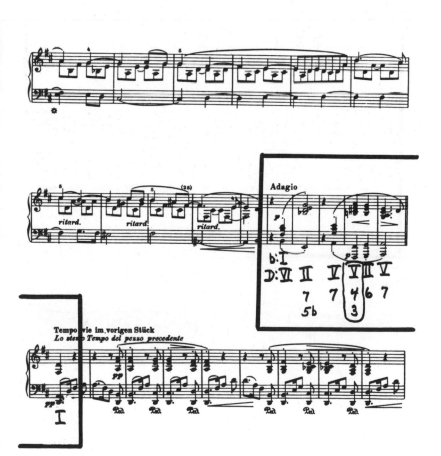

Example Number 48. Robert Schumann, Kreisleriana, Opus 16, Number 6, Volume 3, p. 81.

Example Number 49. Robert Schumann, Faschingsschwank
aus Wien, Opus 26, "Allegro", Volume 4, pp. 136-137.

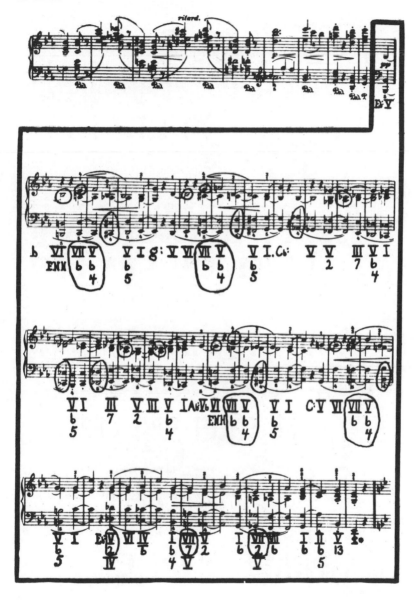

Example Number 50. Robert Schumann, Novelletten, Opus 21, Number 3, Volume 4, p. 45.

obscure the harmony. The soft, swift-moving chords help create an atmosphere of mystery.

In the first three measures of the third movement of the *Phantasie*, Opus 17 (Example 51, p. 124), Schumann creates the effect of mystery and vagueness by not sharply defining a key. Even though the chords can be analyzed in C major, the predominant tonality of the movement, Schumann is more concerned with the downward movement by thirds, i.e., a C major triad, followed by an A major and F major triad. Furthermore, the triads are arpeggiated and played softly, which further intensifies the feeling of vagueness. This impression is also created in the first of the *Nachtstücke*, which was originally titled "Funeral March" (Example 52, p. 125). The piece, which is in C major, begins deceptively on the supertonic. After D minor is tonicized in the first measure and one-half, Schumann cursorily establishes C major, but in measure three, he returns to D minor. Schumann does not finally define C major until measures seven and eight.

A feeling of uncertainty is not only achieved through progressions and cadences, but also through dissolution of the melody and harmony. In Example 53a, p. 126, the melody in line one is dissolved in lines two and three through the omission of one note each time the scale motive is presented until the melody ultimately disappears in silence. Dissolution of harmony is present in the last three bars of Example 53b, p. 126, where Schumann removes chord tones one at a time, leaving only the A before the final cadence.

The subjective, emotionally intoned nuances and differentiations of romantic thought are mirrored in Schumann's harmonic constructions, in his searching for delayed resolutions, and above all in the frequent application of shifting and complicated rhythmic patterns. His technique is a reflection and expression of the inexplicability of cosmic phenomena. In the rationalistic eighteenth century, when philosophers believed they could explain the world completely, a more lucid type of music was composed than in the nineteenth century, when the mysteries of nature were enshrouded in a veil of darkness and uncertainty.

Through shifting rhythms, as well as through harmony, Schumann is able to create this feeling of uncertainty. His piano music contains many examples of compositions filled with unusual and changing rhythms, which are accomplished mainly through rhythmic delays and complexities. In his desire to achieve striking rhythmic effects Schumann may disregard the

Example Number 51. Robert Schumann, Phantasie,
Opus 17, Volume 3, p. 112.

125

Example Number 53 a and b. Robert Schumann, Papillons, Opus 2, Number 12, Volume 1, p. 23.

bar line (Example 54, p. 128). He may achieve a freer rhythmic effect by shifting the accent in order, for example, to make the downbeat fall in the left hand on the last eighth note of the measure instead of over the bar line (Example 55, p. 129).

Special rhythmic subtleties are connected with the use of triple rhythm. In Example 56, p. 130, Schumann vacillates between a duple and triple pulse. Although the piece is written in triple meter, it begins by giving the listener a feeling of duple meter, an impression which is continued by shifting the accent in measure 2, score 1. At the end of measure 5, score 1, measure 5, score 2, and measures 1 and 5, score 5, the feeling of duple meter is repeated.

The device of hemiola is used also by Schumann. According to Willi Apel:

> In treatises on mensural notation (15th, 16th centuries) the term is applied to time-values which are in the relationship of 3:2, particularly to the use of blackened notes in *tempus perfectum*, or, in modern terms, of three half-notes instead of two dotted half-notes.[207]

In Example 57a, p. 131, Schumann writes an implied hemiola in the bass, revealed five measures later by accent marks, which create a triple meter within a notated duple (Example 57b, p. 131). A hemiola is found in Example 58a, p. 132, where a duple meter is implied within a notated triple. The melodic accent and the downward skip of a fourth enhance the two-beat pattern. In Example 58b, p. 132, the same effect is achieved with the addition of a pedal point, which creates a cross accent; in Example 58c, p. 132, the hemiola is expanded by implying a duple meter in the treble and a triple meter in the bass. Although the meter is triple, both hands have separate rhythmic patterns, whose accents do not coincide. Schumann further complicates rhythmic patterns by delaying the melody by one sixteenth note, as well as by writing duple against triple meters (Example 59, p. 133). In Example 60, p. 134, Schumann writes an even more intricate hemiola, which gives the impression of duple meter. Furthermore, the concept of a hemiola has been extended to include harmonic clashes. The harmony in the treble anticipates the chords in the bass. Finally the idea of a hemiola is expanded to include a hemiola with a quadruplet. Schumann writes this rhythmic complexity near the end of the "Préambule" from *Carnaval*, which is written in a triple meter (Example 61, p. 135).

One of the most unusual rhythmic patterns Schumann composes is in "Eusebius" from *Carnaval*, with its use of quintuplets

Example Number 54. Robert Schumann, Faschingsschwank aus Wien, Opus 26, "Allegro", Volume 4, p. 130.

128

Example Number 55. Robert Schumann, <u>Kreisleriana</u>,
Opus 16, Number 8, Volume 3, p. 85.

Example Number 56. Robert Schumann, <u>Novelletten</u>,
Opus 21, Number 5, Volume 4, p. 56.

Example Number 57 a and b.   Robert Schumann, Davidsbündlertänze, Opus 6, Number 6 (First edition), Volume 1, p. 113.

Example Number 58 a, b and c. Robert Schumann, Novelletten, Opus 21, Number 5, Volume 4, p. 57.

Phantasiestücke

Fantastic Pieces   Pièces fantastiques

Fräulein Anna Robena Laidlav gewidmet

Robert Schumann, Op. 12
(1837)

Des Abends
Evening   Au soir

Sehr innig zu spielen M.M. ♪=76
Con molto sentimento

Example Number 60.   Robert Schumann, Davidsbündler,
Opus 6, Number 1 (Second edition), Volume 1, p. 133.

Example Number 61. Robert Schumann, Carnaval, Opus 9, "Préambule", Volume 2, p. 3.

and septuplets (Example 62, p. 137). In measures 1-3 Schumann writes septuplets against two quarter notes; in measures 9 and 10 a quintuplet and a triplet against two quarters; in measure 11 a quintuplet and triplet against a triplet comprising quarter notes; and in measure 12 a quintuplet and two eighths, which are preceded by a grace note, against a triplet comprising quarter notes.

In his attempt to create an aura of mystery and suspense, Schumann employs temporal displacement by means of anticipation and delay of melody and harmony. These two methods are contradictory; if melody is anticipated, it can no longer be delayed and vice versa. Despite this fact, or possibly because of it, if viewed in the light of Hegelian dialectic, Schumann achieves the same effect by means of contradictory methods. Harmony is anticipated in "Etüde VI" of the *Symphonische Etüden*, when a thirty-second note implies the harmony of the following chord (Example 63, p. 138). In Example 64, p. 139, Schumann delays the chord tones in the bass through the use of retardations.

A more complicated use of anticipation and delay is found in the piece "Fast zu ernst" from *Kinderszenen* (Example 65, p. 140). The melody can be reduced to a simpler version, as seen in Example 66, p. 141. By comparing the two forms of the melody, it can be seen that in the original version Schumann has delayed the melody by one-sixteenth note. Through this delay, melodic and harmonic events do not coincide. Furthermore, the anticipations which occur in measures 5 and 6 of the original version (Example 66a, p. 141) produce the dual effect of delaying the melody, and at the same time anticipating the harmony. In the simpler version of the melody (Example 66b, p. 141) these tones are heard as escape notes. Schumann further clouds the harmony by writing nonharmonic tones which can be heard momentarily in a consonant relationship (Example 66a, p. 141, measure 2) and by having harmonic tones appear as if they were nonharmonic (Example 66a, p. 141, measure 4). Through these various rhythmic shiftings and complexities, Schumann is able to create an atmosphere of uncertainty which would have been foreign to many of the more conservative composers of the preceding centuries.

Although Schumann admires the more classic composers, such as Bach, he dislikes having to apply some of their stricter techniques. Apparently in the beginning it was difficult for him to master contrapuntal complexities, and it was not until 1844-1845 that he fully achieved this skill. Although he laments his inability

Example Number 62 a, b, c and d. Robert Schumann, <u>Carnaval</u>, Opus 9, "Eusebius", Volume 2, p. 7.

Example Number 63. Robert Schumann, Symphonische Etüden, Opus 13, Etüde VI, Volume 2, p. 129. (A=Anticipation).

Etüde VI
(Variation V)

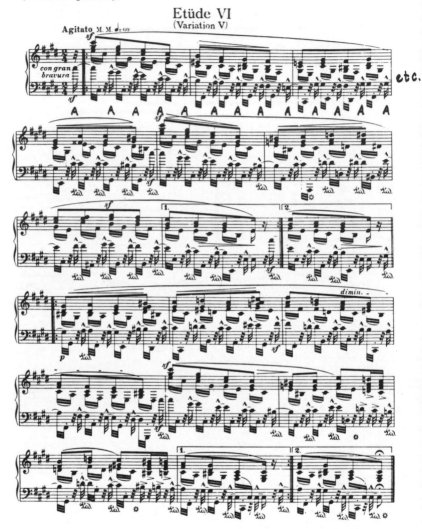

Example Number 64. Robert Schumann, Variationen über
den Namen Abegg, Opus 1, Variation 2, Volume 1, p. 3.
(R=retardation)

Example Number 65. Robert Schumann, Kinderszenen,
Opus 15, "Fast zu ernst", Number 10, Volume 3, p. 53.

Ritter vom Steckenpferd

Knight of the Rocking-Horse   Sur le cheval de bois

Fast zu ernst

Almost too serious   Presque trop sérieux

Example Number 66.

(Ped. =Pedal tone.
 S =Suspension.
 R =Retardation.
 P=Passing tone.
 E=Escape tone.
 A=Anticipation.)

Example 66a.

Example 66b.

141

to produce fugues, he nevertheless recognizes the benefits of this technique of composition. He seriously studied counterpoint under Heinrich Dorn, and writes Wieck in January, 1832:

I can never come to an agreement with Dorn; . . . by a fugue he wants me to understand music. Heavens! How different people are! However, I feel that theoretical studies have had a good influence on me. If formerly everything was an inspiration of the moment, now I look more at the play of my enthusiasm, perhaps sometimes I stand quietly in the center of it in order to look around and see where I am.[208]

Schumann's counterpoint of the 1830s is based on figured harmony more than the interweaving of independent voices. The impression of counterpoint is achieved often through a line harmonized by a rhythmic figure (Example 67, p. 143). Many of the baroque contrapuntal devices influenced Schumann, for example, imitation (Example 68, p. 144). Although this example presents a four-voice texture, the impression of more voices is given, because there are five or six entries. The number of voices is obscured further by their overlappings. He also employs the technique of imitation by inversion (Example 69, p. 145), canon (Example 70, p. 146), chordal canon, which is an expansion of a linear canon (Example 71, p. 147), harmonized canon (Example 72, p. 148), stretto (Example 73, p. 149), and invertible counterpoint (Example 74, p. 150). Furthermore, Schumann uses fugal techniques, as found in the seventh number from *Kreisleriana* with its fugato section (Example 75, p. 151), and the *Fughette*, Opus 32, with its harmonized fugue subject (Example 76, p. 152).

Although through the study of baroque techniques, and more specifically Bach's works, Schumann enlarged his sense of form, he is nevertheless a product of the romantic spirit, which recognized no distinction between form and content. Both grew and evolved inseparably. As Victor Hugo (1802-1885) writes:

An idea . . . has always only one form which suits it, which is its essential form. . . . With the great poets nothing is more inseparable, nothing more consubstantial than the idea and the expression of the idea. Kill the form, and you almost always kill the idea.[209]

Schumann with his strong emphasis on the value of intuitive composition, would have agreed with August Schlegel, who contends that:

. . . such people have no conception that form is much more than a

142

Example Number 67. Robert Schumann, Impromptus, Opus 5,
Number 12 (First edition), Volume 1, p. 89.

Example Number 68. Robert Schumann, Novelletten,
Opus 21, Number 1, Volume 4, p. 32.

*)Hier ist eine zartere Tongebung am Platz.
Here a softer quality of tone is suitable.
Employer ici un toucher plus doux

Example Number 69. Robert Schumann, <u>Novelletten,</u>
Opus 21, Number 2, Volume 4, p. 39.

Example Number 70. Robert Schumann, Papillons, Opus 2, Number 3, Volume 1, p. 13.

Etüde IV
(Variation III)

147

Example Number 72. Robert Schumann, Carnaval, Opus 9, "Reconnaissance", Volume 2, p. 15.

Example Number 73.   Robert Schumann, <u>Intermezzi</u>,
Opus 4, Number 2, Volume 1, p. 58.

Example Number 74. Robert Schumann, Kreisleriana, Opus 16, Number 2, Volume 3, p. 67.

Example Number 75. Robert Schumann, _Kreisleriana_,
Opus 16, Number 7, Volume 3, p. 83.

Example Number 76. Robert Schumann, Scherzo, Gigue,
Romanze und Fughette, Opus 32, Volume 4, p. 183.

Fughette

mould, a convenience for the poet, and equally from the first conception of a poem, content and form are inseparable, as soul and body.[210]

In a letter to Hirschbach, dated September 7, 1838, Schumann
states practically the same sentiment.

You know nothing about my larger compositions, sonatas (which
appeared under Florestan and Eusebius' name). I believe (if you do
not already see it in my shorter pieces) you would see how numerous
and new are the forms contained in them. I do not think about form
any more while composing; I just do it.[211]

Because Schumann strongly supports progressive movements in
music, he naturally praises other composers who strive to create
new forms and criticizes those who do not.

Whoever always works in the same forms and conditions will become
at last a mannerist or Philistine. There is nothing more harmful for
an artist than continued repose in a convenient form; as one grows
older the creative power itself diminishes and then it is too late. Many
a first-rate talent only then recognizes that but half of his problem
was solved.[212]

One of Schumann's major contributions to the history of form
is his creation of a variety of small forms. Schumann's interest in
the development of smaller forms had been stimulated by his
study of Schubert, but it was intensified by the general romantic
enthusiasm to delve in miniatures, as evidenced by the development of the *Lied* and the smaller piano pieces of composers such
as Mendelssohn and Chopin. Schumann considers it more difficult
to write in smaller forms than larger ones; the former demands a
compression of thought and a careful selection of each note. In
1835 he writes the following epigram: "Everything beautiful is
difficult, the short the most difficult." [213] Seven years later he
maintains that:

There are some composers, who, when others need hours, know how
to express themselves in minutes. For the presentation as well as for
the enjoyment of such spiritually concentrated compositions, however, an increased strength is needed on the part of the interpreter
and receivers, and also the appropriate time and place.[214]

In studying Schumann's music from 1830-1840 a transition
from a romantic to a more classic composer can be seen, a trend
which is reflected in his treatment of smaller forms. The earlier
shorter compositions are not as tightly structured as his later
ones. For example, the *Allegro*, Opus 8, composed in 1831, is
improvisatory and rhapsodic in nature with quickly shifting

153

moods and tempi. The *Toccata*, Opus 7 (1832), breathes the same spirit, although it possesses a more structured plan. By 1838, with the composition of the *Arabesque*, Opus 18, and 1839 with the *Blumenstück*, Opus 19, Schumann writes compositions which are more tightly organized. The *Arabesque* is in rondo form; it contains an A section in C major, followed by a B section (Minore I) in E minor, then a return of the A section, followed by a C section containing new material but again in E minor (Minore II), and finally a return of the A section. The *Blumenstück* is also a structured rondo-like piece which follows the pattern: ABCBDEB(A). The last statement of the A section is only suggested in the form of a coda.

A trend from romanticism to classicism cannot be noted so clearly in Schumann's larger compositions of this decade. In *Papillons*, Opus 2 (1830-1831), Schumann bases a series of twelve dances on a scene, a masked ball, from Jean Paul's *Flegeljahre*. Because *Papillons* was written in 1830-1831, at a time when Schumann was writing pieces which were freer in form, for example, the *Allegro*, Opus 8, it might be expected that the individual sections would be rhapsodic and improvisatory, but this is not the case. However, their concise form is due partly to the fact that they are based on previous polonaises and waltzes, which are more classic in form. The *Kinderszenen*, Opus 15 (1838), which have suggestive titles and are not closely related to any particular story, also employ clear cut forms. The *Papillons* are, in one respect, more romantic than the *Kinderszenen*; the former are more closely related to literature than the latter. Although the overall impression of the *Humoresque*, Opus 20 (1839) is kaleidoscopic, the forms of the individual sections are concise. For example, "Mit einigen Pomp" is monothematic, being based on a single rhythmic figure. "Einfach und zart" is in ternary form, and "Einfach" is in *Bogen* form (ABCBA).

In examining the three sets of variations Schumann wrote for piano between 1830-1840, a clearer trend from romanticism toward classicism can be found. The most romantic are the *Variationen über den Namen Abegg*, Opus 1, (1830), which are based on a *soggetto cavato* (ABEGG). The variations are rhapsodic in nature, with the last one entitled "Finale alla Fantasia". The *Impromptus* Opus 5 (1832), which are constructed on a bass melody by Clara Wieck, are less romantic than the Opus 1 variations, being tied to a continuous theme, rather than a *soggetto cavato*. The *Impromptus* are more classic in view of the theme, which is in the form ABB. The structure of the variations in the second edition (1832) is still more organized, including additional repeat marks. The last set of variations Schumann wrote during this period, the *Symphonische Etüden*, Opus 13 (1834), is the most classic. The basis for the variations is neither a *soggetto cavato*, nor a bass theme, but a symmetrical melody comprised of two phrases of eight measures each, which Schumann borrows from Baron von Fricken. Most of the variations follow this regular pattern, although in some cases Schumann extends the phrase lengths, for example, in Etüdes 3, 7, and 9. The last variation, which employs a theme from Marschner's opera *Der Templer und Die Jüdin*, is in rondo form, which follows the general pattern: ABCABCA. The variations are more tightly organized, especially through the use of binary and ternary song forms and repeat marks, more consistent in texture, and less improvisatory than the Opus 1 or Opus 5 variations.

Schumann's concern with smaller forms leads him not only to write shorter individual works, which contain smaller sections, but also larger works which are comprised of miniatures. Although the same general trend from romantic to classic may be seen in these works, they also show a slight reversion to romanticism in 1839. The *Intermezzi*, Opus 4 (1832), are similar in spirit to the *Allegro*, Opus 8, and the *Toccata*, Opus 7, all three works having an improvisatory nature. The *Intermezzi* are Schumann's first attempt at writing in more extended forms. They are episodic in nature, and unifying devices are not prevalent, although in the second "Intermezzo" Schumann uses a short rhythmical figure which recurs at the end of this "Intermezzo" in augmentation, and in diminution in the third "Intermezzo". Only the fourth one has a tightly organized form. Even this "Intermezzo" is constructed around two smaller musical sources, containing a middle section, which is a transcription of one of Schumann's earlier songs.

Carnaval, Opus 9 (1835), is not as loosely organized as the *Intermezzi*, and for this reason not as romantic. In *Carnaval*, Schumann employs a stronger cohesive factor, the structural patterns of ASCH or SCHA, which form a basis for most of the individual sections. Furthermore, themes in one section may appear later in another; for example, the measures marked "Presto", which end the "Préambule", also conclude *Carnaval*.

Although the *Phantasiestücke*, Opus 12 (1837), have romantic titles, they do not possess the programmatic unity of *Carnaval;*

they are rather a series of pieces of contrasting moods. More important, they employ classic forms. "Warum" is in lapidary form, containing symmetrical phrases of eight measures, "Fabel" is in *Bogen* form, and "Grillen" is in rondo form with a development section. The *Davidsbündlertänze*, Opus 6 (1837) and *Kreisleriana*, Opus 16 (1838) are less romantic than the *Phantasiestücke*, not so much in terms of form, but because they are not closely tied to a program. The union of literature and music, which is an integral part of romantic thought, is less evident.

Even though the *Novelletten*, Opus 21 (1838) appear similar to the *Intermezzi*, since both works contain separate pieces, there is one important difference. The individual pieces contained within the *Novelletten* employ more tightly organized forms than those in the *Intermezzi*. For example, Number 2 of the *Novelletten* is an expanded ternary form, with the B section labeled "Intermezzo", and Number 7 is a rondo. Even Number 8, which appears improvisatory, has the following form: A, B (Trio I), A, C (Trio II), cadenza, DED, FGHGF (a *Bogen* form), C.

Although Schumann employs classic forms in his piano works of the late 1830s, a slight reversion to romanticism is present. For example, the *Nachtstücke*, Opus 23 (1839) bear a programmatic title, and the *Faschingsschwank aus Wein*, Opus 26 (1840) is unified by a spirit of carnival time. The four pieces in *Nachtstücke* were originally called "Funeral March", "Strange Company", "Nocturnal Carousal", and "Rondo with Two Voices". A tinge of romanticism also is noted in Schumann's titling pieces *Blumenstück*, and *Drei Romanzen*, both of which were written in 1839.

In addition to his awareness of the importance of smaller forms, Schumann's genius also lies in the extension of his ideas through standard genre, for example, the sonata. In his famous criticism of the *Symphonie Fantastique*, Schumann lauds Berlioz's invention of new forms. Although he had little personal contact with Berlioz, Schumann feels an attraction to him and subsequently includes him in his imaginary group of *Davidsbündler*. Schumann regrets the audience's inability to understand the meaning of Berlioz's unique manner of expression.

The reason for the unfortunate misunderstanding seems really to lie in the new expression, in the unusual [nature] of this new form. Most people, on the first or second hearing, stick to details too much. It is like reading a difficult handwriting; he who stops at every single word when deciphering needs incomparably more time than he who initially skims through all of it in order to get to know the sense and the purpose. Besides, as already intimated, nothing arouses more displeasure and contradiction than a new form which carries an old name. . . . The more singular and artistic a work obviously appears to be, the more cautiously it should be judged.[215]

In his criticism of Berlioz's *Symphonie Fantastique*, Schumann describes the difference between Berlioz's use of the sonata form and the norm, as demonstrated in the diagram on page 158.[216]

In an examination of Schumann's sonatas, the move from romanticism to classicism is less evident. First of all, the sonata is basically a classic form; and, secondly, the sonatas were all written at about the same time. The *Sonata in F sharp Minor*, Opus 11, was composed in 1833-1835, the *Sonata in F Minor*, Opus 14, in 1836, the *Phantasie*, Opus 17, which is actually a sonata, because of its formal structure, in 1836, and the *Sonata in G Minor*, Opus 22, in 1835-1838. None of these works are tightly organized, or give the impression of being compact, unified structures. The *Phantasie*, Opus 17, is perhaps the most romantic in form, especially since it ends with a slow movement. The first movement, which is in sonata-allegro form, lacks a development section; instead Schumann has added an interlude, "Im Legendenton", which is built on a transformation of one of the themes of the exposition. The whole work has a programmatic tinge, implied by the poem of Friedrich Schlegel which precedes it.

The *Sonata*, Opus 11, also has certain traits which deviate from the accustomed pattern and make it a romantic sonata. For example, the introduction to the first movement gives the impression of an improvisation, and a reminiscence of the motive used in the introduction appears just before the recapitulation in the first movement; the second movement is based on a previously composed song; the return of the scherzo in the third movement is shortened; and the fourth movement contains a lengthened coda, rather than a development section. In this fourth movement a self-contained interlude, which has a folklike nature, appears where a development section might have been expected. However, the *Sonata*, Opus 11, is more classic than the *Phantasie*, because it follows a more traditional format, that is, a first movement in sonata-allegro form, a slow movement in ternary form, a third movement in an expanded ternary form (*Scherzo ed Intermezzo*), and a fourth movement in a general sonata-allegro form.

Although the *Sonata*, Opus 14, contains divergencies from

Berlioz's Conception of Sonata Form
(as analyzed by R. Schumann)

First Theme
(G-Major)

Development
sections with
a second theme.

Development
sections with
a second theme.

First Theme
(C-Major) End.
(C-Major)

Beginning.
(C-Major)

First Theme
(C-Major) . . . .
(G-Major, E-Minor) . . . . (E-Minor, G-Major)

Schumann's Conception of the Norm

Development
(A-Minor)
(Reworking of
two themes)

First Theme
(C-Major)

First Theme
(C-Major) . . . .

Second
(G-Major) . . . .

Second
(C-Major)

strict classic form, such as the repetition of the development section in the recapitulation of the first movement, it is less romantic than the *Sonata*, Opus 11, especially in view of the revision Schumann made of the *Sonata*, Opus 14, in 1853. He changed many passages to accommodate the fingers and to meet the acoustical requirements of the concert hall, and he added the second movement, a scherzo, to give the work a more classic format. Furthermore, he employs a variation technique in the second movement, a classic device.

The *Sonata*, Opus 22, also has romantic traits. For example, Schumann anticipates the tonic key, G minor, in the development section of the first movement, the scherzo is unclassically brief, and the coda of the last movement is marked "Quasi cadenza". Nevertheless, it follows the rules of classic form more than any of the other three works. It contains a first movement which is in sonata-allegro form, a second which is a set of variations based on a song, a third which is a short scherzo, and a fourth in rondo form. The variations in the second movement are more classic than the treatment of the song in the *Sonata*, Opus 11.[217]

Although he employs many different forms in his piano music, for example, dance patterns (waltz, minuet, polonaise, gigue), rondo, scherzo and trio, air and variations, and sonata, Schumann is adventurous in not conforming to the expected specifications. From knowledge of his sketchbooks, of his standards for evaluating other composers, and of his manner of writing, it is apparent that he often composed intuitively. But Schumann should not be taken too literally when he advises composers to create without much reflection, for he carefully worked out the details of his music. For him the form of a work evolved out of the material, which was a natural outgrowth of his basic improvisatory and intuitive approach to composition. "The form is the chalice of the spirit." [218] "The task is to spiritualize matter so that in the process everything material will be forgotten." [219]

Schumann's principles and methods of composition are rooted in his aesthetics and theoretical background. He complains about traditional composers who never try anything new, and believes that the artist who is a conformist will be forgotten during the course of history. The important thing for Schumann is that the original personality must dominate.

And so it often occurred that those who . . . wanted to swim against the stream, had to continue their way lonely and without acclaim, while those who compromised, soon giving up loftier aspirations, swam with hundreds of others in the stream and disappeared without a trace.[220]

For Schumann, the artist must remain true to his own convictions. By persevering in his principles, the original genius achieves a more satisfying personal triumph than one who bends his principles to the popular whim. Schumann points out how Beethoven exemplified the man of integrity.

German composers fail most often in their intention of wanting to please the public. If only one would produce something original, simple, deeply sensuous, completely from within himself, he would find out whether he would not gain more. Whoever always meets the public with outstretched arms usually will be looked down upon. When Beethoven walked around with his head bent and arms crossed, then the mob meekly dispersed, and gradually even his unusual language became more familiar to them.[221]

Finally, on this point of artistic integrity, Schumann thinks that the true artist should express his own thoughts and ideas sincerely, and be content with the knowledge of his own achievement and the acclaim of his peers. "Little depends on the greater or lesser [degree] of outward acclaim. You must feel the reward within yourself, in the recognition by artists, . . ." [222]

CHAPTER VI

SCHUMANN ON PROGRAMMATIC MUSIC

The interplay of music and literature assumes a predominating role in a discussion of programmatic music. Music without poetic ideas is for many romantics unthinkable. The romantic composer E. T. A. Hoffmann, for instance, believes that music presents occurrences of the outside world by means of awakening emotions through its mysterious language.[223]

Other composers, for example, Carl Maria von Weber, also are interested in the interrelationship between words and music. For Weber music is the outward expression of man's passions. It is an abstract conception in contrast to the more definite relationship between words and the external world. Weber believes exact correlations should not be sought.

What love is to man, music is to the arts, as well as to man, for it is truly love itself, the purest, most ethereal language of the passions, containing a thousandfold perpetually changing colors for all shades of emotions, . . . but understood simultaneously by a thousand persons of differing sensibility.[224]

In his diary, in 1832, Schumann expresses his idea on the relationship between music and literature.

I said to Wieck: people are accustomed to find in music either happiness or pain. . . . Passionate moments pass by the less sensitive uncomprehended, indeed even despised. I prove that with Schubert and Beethoven. Why should there not be an opera without text, that would be equally dramatic? [225]

Schumann refuses to enchain the listener's mind by demanding adherence to a definite program. The imagination of the listener is at liberty to form any association appropriate. The question logically arises, of what importance is a title to Schumann? The musical content is of primary importance, and he believes that the titles should not be distracting. As he indicates in his criticism of Berlioz's *Symphonie Fantastique,* the listener should not be directed beyond a certain point.

Whether this [music] will awaken now similar images, to [those] he

161

wanted to draw, in someone who does not know the intention of the composer, I, who read the program before listening, cannot decide. Once the eye has been guided to one point, the ear no longer judges independently.[226]

Perhaps for this reason he tries to suppress the titles which he originally intended for the four movements of his *B flat Symphony* ("Spring") and two of the movements of his *E flat Symphony* ("Rhenish").

Furthermore, he names most of his pieces after they are conceived musically. This does not imply that in Schumann's mind the literary connotations are not present simultaneously with his composition of the pieces or even before they are conceived, but it does indicate the relative value he attaches to a title. Eugenie Schumann, his daughter, claims that the titles are not necessary to a musical understanding of his works, but that if one is conscious of them, they can serve as an aid to a more complete appreciation of the composition. "Father thought up the titles for the pieces only after they were completed. They are very pertinent and can facilitate the understanding, but necessary they are not."[227]

Misunderstanding may arise as to the meaning of the term "necessary" [*nötig*], because Schumann claims that titles are not essential. But what is meant here by the word "necessary"? A title is important in comprehending the piece on other planes than the musical, and furthermore, if a composer is careful in choosing a name for a piece, he can capture a whole story or mood. The creator has the power to steer the listener's imagination into clearer waters. Schumann writes:

. . . that a well-chosen sign always enhances the hotel and the store, and that the crowd can be nourished not only with bread, but also with words. Titles, therefore, are necessary to us for our work. . . . I simply choose a meaningful title which has both validity and significance for the whole story.[228]

One of the best proofs that Schumann is concerned with the captions he attaches to pieces is found in the sketchbooks for *Album für die Jugend*, where he wants to direct the listener's imagination. He changes the names until they precisely express his intentions; for example, the piece "Erster Verlust" (First Sorrow) was called "Kinderunglück" (Child's Misfortune) in the sketchbook, and "Armes Waisenkind" (Poor Orphan Child) was previously titled "Armes Bettlerkind" (Poor Beggar Child).[229] But if he finds a suitable title, it helps to establish a general mood rather than point out particular instances.

Why should it be so astonishing when good friends sit together, and the composer plays something for them, and [they], as if touched by a ray of light, suddenly exclaim: "Should not this or that piece be given an appropriate title and by that, would the opus not be indescribably enhanced?" And the composer rejoices and in capital letters gives titles to the pieces concerned. The titles under consideration probably are not based on a deeper reason; the music was present before the title and completes in flowing melody what this [title] suggests.[230]

Because the musical content of a piece is of primary importance, the title is not a prerequisite for understanding the composition on a musical level. "The main point remains whether music in itself, without words and commentary, is the thing, and preferably whether the spirit [of music] dwells within." [231]

Although Schumann titles his pieces after they are written, it is inconsequential to him whether the musical or literary idea appears first, as is shown in a criticism of Sterndale Bennett's Opus 10, where Schumann states that composers often are unconscious of the influence of extramusical sensations, ideas, and impressions.

In what way, incidentally, the sketches originated, whether from the internal to the external or vice versa, does not matter and no one can decide. Usually composers themselves do not know; one [composition] originates like this, the other like that; often an external picture points the way, often a sequence of tones conjures up [an external picture]. If only music and independent melody remain, one should not brood but enjoy it.[232]

Although the music is the most essential element in a composition, Schumann believes that outside influences which affect the composer at the moment of creation should be taken into consideration. Literary ideas, he continues, are often hints which stimulate the composer's musical inspiration.

As to the difficult question in general, to what extent instrumental music may go in presenting thoughts and events, here many seem too scrupulous. It is certainly wrong to believe that composers take up pen and paper with the torturous intention of expressing, of portraying, of painting this or that. Yet outward accidental influences and impressions should not be underestimated. Unconsciously along with the musical image [*Phantasie*] an idea continues to operate along with the ear, the eye; and this, the ever active organ, perceives among the sounds and tones certain contours which may solidify and assume the shape of clear cut figures. The more the elements contain within themselves thoughts and forms produced by tones related to music, the more poetic or graphic expression the composition will have; the more fantastically or acutely the musician perceives in general, the more his work will uplift and captivate. Why should the thought of immortality not occur to Beethoven in the midst of his improvising [*Phantasie*]? Why should the memory of a mighty fallen hero not inspire him to a work? Why should the memory of a blissfully spent moment not [*occur*] to another? Or do we wish to be ungrateful to Shakespeare for having evoked from the breast of a young composer a work worthy of him,—ungrateful to nature, and deny that we borrowed from her beauty and serenity for our works? Italy, the Alps, the image of the ocean, a spring twilight—should music have not told us anything about all these? [233]

As a youth Schumann amused his friends by characterizing them through improvisations at the piano, and then asking them to guess the persons represented. The technique was transferred into his piano music, especially as demonstrated in *Carnaval*. Characters from a carnival appear in the guise of "Pierrot", the sad clown, "Arlequin", his counterpart, "Coquette", the *ingénue*, and "Pantalon et Colombine", the quarreling lovers. The two sides of Schumann's personality appear in the characters of "Eusebius" and "Florestan". Schumann also depicts real people, for example, Clara in "Chiarina", Ernestine von Fricken in "Estrella", Chopin, Paganini, and the whole *Davidsbund* in the "Marche des 'Davidsbündler' contre les Philistins". Schumann also has a predilection to recognize characters in the music of other composers, which he does subjectively but consciously in the review of Chopin's *Variations on 'La ci darem la mano'*, Opus 2. He respects Chopin for being able to characterize different persons so convincingly that they are recognizable to him, although he does not conclude that everyone who hears the variations will have similar reactions; the implication is that those with imagination and fantasy may.

Eusebius said, Don Giovanni, Zerlina, Leporello . . . would be the performing characters of the variations. The first would be distinguished, courtly, seductive, and splendid; the second, indeed, more intimate, quarrelsome, comical and vivacious, . . . the third, reminiscent of moonlight . . . As subjective as I believe all this may be, and as little as Chopin certainly may have intended, I still bow my head to his genius, to his firm endeavor. . . , to his diligence and his imagination.[234]

Schumann believes that music is enhanced through poetic ideas, and he adheres to an *Inhaltsästhetik* (the aesthetic concerning beauty and form of content) to the extent that his compositions are enlightened by the addition of a literary element. For Schumann, music cannot reproduce a story, but can recapture its atmosphere, an idea which is shown in "Im Legendenton" of the *Phantasie*, Opus 17, or in "Die Fabel" from the *Phantasiestücke*, Opus 12. In the section from the *Phantasie*, Schumann instructs the performer to play as if he were telling a story. "Die Fabel" is an example of Schumann's desire to give the impression of a fairytale. In neither piece does Schumann attempt to relate a definite story, but rather to create a mood.

He seems to affirm the unity of the musical and literary imagination which many other composers, who limit themselves more to absolute music, find irreconcilable. In his conception of the relationship between music and poetry, Schumann is influenced greatly by Jean Paul.[235] Often Schumann discovers an avenue of approach to Jean Paul through the music of other composers. At the home of his friend Carus he heard songs of Wiederbein, after which he remarks:

Through these I learned to understand and decipher Jean Paul's veiled words, Jean Paul's dark spiritual tones [*Geistertöne*] first became understandable and clear to me through that magical clothing of its tonal creations.[236]

Furthermore, Schumann recognizes his great debt to Jean Paul.

I often ask myself what would have become of me if I had never known Jean Paul: in one respect at any rate he seems to have an affinity with me, for I foresaw him. . . . Perhaps I would have written the same kind of poetry . . . but I would have withdrawn myself less from other people and dreamt less. I cannot decide, really, what would have become of me, the problem is impossible to work out.[237]

In a letter dated March 7, 1828, Schumann ranks him as the greatest author.

Jean Paul still ranks highest with me, and I place him above all, not even with the exception of Schiller, (Goethe I do not yet understand).[238]

Ten years later he advises Clara to read Jean Paul, and especially *Flegeljahre*, cautioning her to have patience, because at first it will appear confusing; later she will recognize the inner logic which underlies the great web of fantasy.

Then I ask you, do read sometime in Jean Paul, *Die Flegeljahre* first; at the start one must go through some thickets and stunted undergrowth—then, however, what a divine heart will unfold itself to you! [239]

One of the most important concepts which Schumann derives

from Jean Paul is the idea of a double nature [*Doppelnatur*]. Based upon an introspective self-analysis, Jean Paul discovers within himself two conflicting personalities, which he mirrors in his novels through the characters Albano and Schoppe, Siebenkäs and Liebgeber, Walt and Vult, Gustav and Flenk, or Flamin and Victor. A very significant pair for Schumann is Walt and Vult; he bases *Papillons* on the "Larventanz" from *Flegeljahre,* in which Walt and Vult vie for the love of Wina. Schumann writes in May, 1828:

> Only the unique Jean Paul could combine in himself two such different characters—he unites many sharp oppositions, although possibly not extremes, in his work and in himself—and still it is only he alone.[240]

Concerning Jean Paul's conception of *Doppelnatur,* René Wellek writes:

> He himself prominently used the theme of the "double" in his novels, as he had a vivid consciousness of man seeing himself, doubling, splitting up into two egos, the one acting, the other observing. In his novels a man is terrified by his own image in a mirror, meets his double, makes his wax figure, looks at his own body and asks: "Somebody is sitting there and I am in him. Who is that?"[241]

In Schumann's writings the idea of a character with two opposing sides first appears in his novel fragment *Selene,* written in 1826. Schumann conceives of himself as the main character, Gustav, and writes the following description of him:

> Gustav—that wild harmonic combination of strength and mildness. It is Gustav's nature to be reserved. Doubt, zest for action, despair—still he remains a whole. . . . He is a painter and poet, and in fact a poet of musical composition [*Tondichter*].[242]

The two sides of Schumann are crystallized later in the figures of Florestan, who represents the personification of poetic illumination and tempestuousness, and Eusebius, who represents the withdrawn and melancholy. A comprehension of the two opposing sides of Schumann's personality is necessary not only for an understanding of him, but also for a deeper appreciation of his piano music. He describes Florestan and Eusebius in the following words:

> Florestan is one of those rare musical persons, who have long before, as it were, anticipated everything to come, everything new and extraordinary; a moment later, the unusual to them is no longer unusual; in a moment the unaccustomed becomes their possession.

166

Eusebius, on the other hand, is dreamy [*schwärmerisch*], as well as calm . . . also his studies are stricter, and his execution at the keyboard more contemplative, but also more delicate and technically closer to perfection than that of Florestan's.[243]

In the same article Schumann compares Florestan and Eusebius, from a slightly different angle.

. . . with his soft hand [Eusebius] quickly discovers the beauties of a work, which also he often uses to cover up mistakes; likewise Florestan possesses a remarkable refinement for recognizing deficiencies instantly. Both of them concern themselves . . . with poetry in which the fantastic element predominates.[244]

One of the best musical portrayals of these two parts of Schumann's nature appears in the fifth and sixth pieces of *Carnaval*, Opus 9. After each one of his *Davidsbündlertänze* he writes either the initials F. (Florestan), E. (Eusebius) or F. and E., when the characters of the separate dances are correlated with either or both of the two quasi-fictitious persons.

Although Schumann attaches programmatic titles to some of his piano compositions, he believes that the power of music lies in its ability to evoke abstract emotions or moods. He recognizes its potential to represent profound emotions, an idea he expresses in a letter dated April 29, 1834, to Theodor Mundt.

It is precisely from music that philosophers could learn that it is possible to say the profoundest things in the world while preserving the appearance of frivolous youthful levity; for that is just what music does when, pretending to be a playing child with a brimfull heart that it is almost ashamed to reveal to the wise and learned, it mischievously hides behind its tinkling musical figures . . . with wonderful sound-meanings which knock at every human heart with the quiet question 'Do you understand me?', but are by no means understood by everyone.[245]

According to Schumann, tones are incapable of painting anything which is not previously associated with them; but, as he writes in 1829, tones have the ability to activate abstract emotions, which in turn conjure up previous experiences in the listener.

Tones all by themselves actually cannot paint anything which emotion has not painted before; if I think about my childhood or the year 1826, A minor and similar keys come to mind, if I think about last September, it dissolves itself as if of its own accord in hard, dissonant pianissimo notes. Whatever occurs to [the composer], he seeks to express through tones.[246]

Schumann also comments on music's ability to evoke isolated images.

The more specific a composition is, the more individual pictures on the whole it unfolds to the listener, the more it captures and the more eternal and new it will be for all times.[247]

There is no mention in the above quotation of a distinct correlation between a specific situation and a musical composition; Schumann does not exclude the possibility of a work containing special private meanings which a listener is not expected to recognize, and he realizes that literary associations may be identified with specific compositions.

Even smaller, more specific pictures can lend such a charming, enduring character, that one is surprised how it [music] can express such features. Thus a composer explained to me, that while composing the picture of a butterfly perpetually appeared, which swam along on a leaf in the brook; this gave to the small piece a delicacy and naïvete as perhaps only the image may possess in reality.[248]

For Schumann, the true test of whether a composer is successful with his illustrative intentions is to give the listener a composition which is filled with programmatic associations and see if he can discover them. Schumann believes that at best only the emotion can be recognized, as is stated in his review of Ludwig Spohr's symphony, *The Consecration of Tones*.

If a listener could be found who, uninformed about the poem and titles of the symphony's individual movements, could give us an account of the pictures which they arouse in him, then this would be a test as to whether the composer had successfully completed his task. . . . Beethoven well knew the risk which he ran with the *Pastoral Symphony*. In the few words "more expression of the emotion than painting", which he placed before it, lies a whole aesthetic for composers.[249]

The philosophic aspect of Schumann's thought is reflected in his conceptions of programmatic music. By examining four representative works, *Papillons, Carnaval, Kinderszenen,* and *Kreisleriana* a trend from a romantic to a more classic style of composing can be noted. In a chronological study of the four compositions a decreasing dependency on literature can be seen. The romantic conception of a union of words and music plays a much less important role in *Kreisleriana* than in *Papillons.* Throughout Schumann's programmatic piano pieces many of his personal experiences are translated into musical terms, although listeners are not expected to grasp the inner meanings. To the romantics, art is a subjective matter, and it is not of primary importance whether all programmatic connotations are understandable.

The programmatic structure of *Papillons* is foreshadowed in the trios of his *Polonaisen* which form the basis for *Papillons*, and have titles such as *la douleur, la belle patrie, la paix, la reconciliation, l'aimable, la fantasie, la serenade.* In Wolfgang Gertler's book, *Robert Schumann in seinen frühen Klavierwerken*, there is an extensive analysis of the relationship between the *Polonaisen*, which date from 1828, and *Papillons*, which were written between 1829 and 1831. Gertler points out that on the whole Schumann borrows figures and phrases which could be blended into a single unified composition.

During the early part of his life Schumann was influenced by the more classical forms, such as the polonaise, but between 1830-1840 he is more affected by romantic trends. It is not surprising to find that the *Polonaisen*, which have classical roots, are transformed into the romantic *Papillons*. Furthermore, Gertler contends that the version Schumann first projected contained a set of *Sechs Walzer* (1829-1830), which correspond to the published version of *Papillons* as follows: Waltz Number 4 = Papillon 6, Waltz Number 5 = Papillon 7, and Waltz Number 6 = Papillon 1. Theodore Töpken, a friend of Schumann's, writes the following concerning Number 8, which was originally part of this series of waltzes:

One number of *Papillons,* Number 8, was originally in D minor. In this key he played it for me first (spring, 1830), and in truth, he said it was a Schubert waltz, which pleased me then very much. I can still see Schumann, enjoying himself like a child, when he succeeded with this mystification.[250]

The source for the title of *Papillons* lies in the romantic conception of a masked ball, which appeals to Schumann because of its mystic symbolism. For the romantic the masked ball is a symbol of illusion and aspiration. The mask itself is a sort of prison, but at the same time it possesses a magic character, which moulds the wearer into the character of his disguise. As Marcel Brion expresses it:

Undoubtedly the masked ball, half real, half fantastic, in which people by their very dissimulation betray their inner natures, exerted a strange fascination for Schumann. It is of all themes the most romantic, expressing as it does the duality of human nature, the uncertainty of man concerning himself, and the haunting fear of the *Doppelgänger,* . . .[251]

The idea of a masked ball is found not only in *Papillons*, but also in *Faschingsschwank aus Wien, Ballszenen, Kinderball*, and to a certain degree, *Carnaval*, which reflects the same spirit and yet is more than a masked ball.

The figure of a butterfly, which was a popular disguise at carnivals, is a masquerade used by Schumann to conceal the idea of a masked ball. Unfortunately, there is not direct evidence which can be correlated with the origins of *Papillons* and butterflies; but a letter written to his mother dated May, 1832, is concerned with the mystic effect of butterflies on Schumann.

In many a sleepless night I saw a distant picture like a goal—while writing down *Papillons*, I really feel how a certain independence tends to develop itself, which, however, the critic usually rejects. —Now the butterflies flutter in the wide heavenly world of spring, spring itself is at the door and looks at me—a child with heavenly blue eyes—and now I begin to understand my existence—the silence is broken.[252]

When he writes to Theodore Töpken, April 5, 1833, he states that the *Papillons* are far more than just a mirror of butterflies.

Number II consists of six measures of introduction and of twelve rhapsodic movements, some shorter, some longer, in changing keys, tempi and rhythms; mostly jesting, fickle and coquettish, a reflection of the nature of butterflies.—(*Papillons* are supposed to be something quite different; in the next letter you will receive the key for the understanding of them.)[253]

Because Schumann is affected by everything in the world around him, there are perhaps many intimate personal experiences contained within *Papillons* which he does not intend to be understood by outsiders.

The literary background to *Papillons* can be found in three letters, in which Schumann links the composition to the next to last chapter in Jean Paul's *Flegeljahre*, called "Der Larventanz" (Masked Ball). Actually Schumann refers mistakenly to this as the last chapter of Jean Paul's novel. The first letter was written to his family April 17, 1832.

The weather today is so scented and heavenly that I can wish for nothing but a carriage entwined with roses, driven homeward on gold and silver threads by a host of butterflies. Then I would say to them: "Carry off the *Papillons* to Therese, Rosalie, and Emilie; flutter and rejoice around them as freely and blissfully as you will; tell my old dear mother something of my dreams and thoughts of my silence". . . . Then ask them all to read as soon as possible the closing scene of Jean Paul's *Flegeljahre*, and tell them that *Papillons* was intended to turn this masked ball into music. Then ask them if they

170

do not perhaps find faithfully reflected in the *Papillons* something of Wina's angelic love, of Walt's poetic nature, and of Vult's swift-flashing soul.[254]

In the second letter, which was written two days later to Rellstab, the Viennese critic, Schumann makes the same point but in a different way.

Not so much for the editor of *Iris*, but rather for the poet and him spiritually akin to Jean Paul, I allow myself to add a few words about the origin of *Papillons*, since the thread which should bind them together is hardly visible. You, honored one, remember the last scene of *Flegeljahre*—masked ball—Walt—Vult—masks—confessions—anger—revelations—hurrying off—concluding scene, and then the departing brother. I kept turning over the last page again and again, for the end seemed to me only a new beginning—almost unconsciously I found myself at the piano, and so one Papillon after another came into being.[255]

The phrases which are particularly important are his claiming *Flegeljahre* and *Papillons* to be "spiritually akin", and also his maintaining that the strand which binds the two is strong, although "hardly visible".

The third letter is dated summer, 1834, and is addressed to his good friend Frau Henriette Voigt, wherein he again mentions *Flegeljahre* and extends his argument by discussing his attempt to set the "words to music".

If you have a spare moment, I pray you read the last chapter of *Flegeljahre*, where everything is there in black and white even to the giant's boot in F sharp minor (at the end of *Flegeljahre*, I feel as if the play were concluded, but as if the curtain did not drop). I say again that I set the words to music, not the reverse, otherwise it seems to me "a silly procedure". Only the ending, while playful coincidence formed as an answer to the beginning, was awakened by Jean Paul.[256]

The most conclusive evidence which could be brought forth to show a connection between the "Larventanz" and *Papillons* is Schumann's copy of *Flegeljahre* in which he marked passages which he wants to illustrate in his music. If one looks, for example, at the words of Jean Paul which are to accompany the fifth number of *Papillons*, and then attempts to relate them to the delicate and intimate piece in G minor, a similarity of moods can be detected (Example 77, pp. 172-173).

Now he stood for a second alone by the tranquil maiden, and the half rose and lily of her face looked out from the half-mask as from the flower-sheath of a drooping bud. Like foreign spirits from two far cosmic nights they looked at each other behind the dark

171

Example Number 77. Robert Schumann, <u>Papillons</u>,
Opus 2, Number 5, Volume 1, pp. 14-15.

masks, like the stars in a solar eclipse, and each soul saw the other from a great distance.[257]

The *Papillons* possibly could have originated as improvisations, suggested by the reading of Jean Paul's *Flegeljahre*. In any event, Schumann attempts to create the mood of a dance, which would be appropriate for "Larventanz", Jean Paul's masked ball. Schumann uses *Flegeljahre* as a source of inspiration for *Papillons*, and as an aid which may help to clarify the meaning of the music. The program aids in creating the atmosphere which Schumann wants his public to feel. However, it is not his aim to depict all details of the story so specifically that the listener may recognize them easily.

For Schumann purely musical considerations are more important than pictorial ones. He attempts to achieve contrasting moods in *Papillons*, as evidenced by the following two facts: first of all, the trios of the *Polonaisen*, which were incorporated into *Papillons*, have different titles suggesting moods; secondly, in his *Tagebuch* of 1831, he discusses the quick changes of atmosphere he achieved throughout the piece.

The impression of a piece should not be doubtful. . . . And who expects of the hearer, when a piece is played to him for the first time, that he shall analyze it in mechanical or harmonic detail?—With the *Papillons* perhaps one could make an exception, since the change is too quick, the colors are too motley and the listener still has the previous page in his head while the player has already finished.[258]

The sections of the work contain a variety of moods. The first is a leisurely waltz, followed by a rapid dance. The canonic third section which follows is heavier than the light and soft dance which comes after it, and the intimate fifth section is followed by a syncopated and dance-like sixth. A more intimate mood is created in the seventh section which is contrasted with a robust dance in the eighth. The ninth section is similar in spirit to the restless second, and the tenth is comprised of various melodies which are folk-like in nature. The eleventh is a Polonaise pastiche, and the twelfth contains a folk dance, a folk-like *Nachtanz*, and finally a reminiscence of the first section of *Papillons*.

Whereas *Papillons* is related to a story and has no title but nevertheless programmatic implications, *Carnaval* has captions which are not related to a story but to the mood of carnival time. For these reasons, *Carnaval* is less romantic than *Papillons*. Like *Papillons*, although not to the same extent, *Carnaval* is the product of long thought and much experimentation. The kernel of the work, for which three different sketches exist, is a set of variations on Schubert's *Sehnsuchtswalzer*. Apparently from all these drafts Schumann preserved only one variation, which eventually takes the shape of the first twenty-four measures of "Préambule".

The *soggetto cavato* ASCH is the unifying device for *Carnaval*. It takes the form either of four notes, A, E flat, C, B or three notes, A flat, C, B. The twenty-one pieces, comprising the final edition of *Carnaval*, are not the only compositions in which he uses ASCH, for Schumann wrote five additional pieces which he withdrew from *Carnaval*, and held in reserve for later publication. One of these, a waltz, became the third of the *Fünf Albumblätter*, published under the title *Bunte Blätter*, Opus 99, in 1852. The other four appeared two years later as numbers 4, 11, 15, and 17 of the *Albumblätter*, Opus 124. The waltz, Number 4, which is in A minor, properly makes use of an enharmonic D sharp in place of E flat. Inasmuch as *Carnaval* centers around flat key signatures, the rejection of this waltz from the final edition of *Carnaval* on the grounds of tonality is understandable. The "Romanza" in B flat, Number 11, emphasizes the ASCH motive by stating it in octaves; it may have been rejected because its middle section is too similar to that of "Reconnaissance". The Waltz in A flat, Number 15, which was rejected, has no definite ASCH connections. Number 17 of the *Albumblätter*, Opus 124, "Elfe", was originally a sketch for *Papillons;* although it contains ASCH, there is no evidence that it ever was intended for inclusion in *Carnaval*.

Musically *Carnaval* and *Papillons* are linked in three ways: first, by the quotation from *Papillons* in "Florestan"; second, by the ninth piece which bears the name "Papillons"; and third, by the last number, the "Marche des 'Davidsbündler' contre les Philistins", where a quotation of the "Grossvatertanz" appears, as in the last number of *Papillons*. In other respects *Carnaval* is an extension of *Papillons*, for both are masked balls.

A masked ball . . . is perhaps the most perfect medium through which poetry can interpret life. In the same way that the poet conceives all conditions and seasons as being of equal worth, all outer phenomena as mere trappings, but all inner qualities as air and sound, the human being seeks in the masked ball to poetise both his very self and life as a whole.[259]

As is shown by the titles to *Carnaval*, which appeared after the composition had been written, Schumann may have found a semblance between his own preconceived musical ideas and the characters he represents. The following quotation from a letter addressed to Moscheles, dated September 22, 1837, about two years after he finished *Carnaval*, indicates that the essence of the music lies in the moods it seeks to convey.

I attached the titles afterwards. Is not music always in itself sufficient and expressive? "Estrella" is a name, such as is placed under portraits, to grasp the picture more firmly; "Reconnaissance" a lover's meeting [*Erkennungsscene*], "Aveu" a confession of love, "Promenade", a walk, as one does at German balls arm in arm with his ladyfriend. All of this certainly does not have any artistic value; the manifold different states of the soul alone seem to me of interest.[260]

And to help the outsider better understand the general trend of his thinking, because the moods change rapidly, he writes suggestive words above the single numbers.

However, some titles, for example, "Chopin" and "Paganini", may have been attached at the time of their conception, since they so aptly fit the pieces. Both "Chopin" and "Paganini" capture the musical style of the two masters and are unlike other Schumann pieces. A title like "Florestan" may have been added to the piece when it was composed, because of its passionate nature and reminiscence of *Papillons*. Finally, there are titles in *Carnaval* which, by themselves, do not seem to fit the mood of the accompanying pieces, for example, "Papillons". In this piece the music does not suggest butterflies, but perhaps people at a masked ball costumed as butterflies.

Carnaval not only has the extramusical connotations associated with the individual pieces, but also those connected with the letters ASCH. The ASCH motive serves as a mask for himself and Ernestine von Fricken. In a letter to Frau Henriette Voigt, Schumann describes his connection with Ernestine von Fricken and the spelling of the name of the small Bohemian town Asch, which had an important influence on the piece.

What do you think of my funny postscript? . . . to which I add the wish, that you (besides others), may sometimes like to play the scale in E-flat [Es], C, B [H] perhaps also A. For I have just found out that Asch is a very musical name for a city, that the same letters lie in my name and are the only musical ones in it, as the following figure shows, which, by the way, greets you kindly. . . .

Example 78.[261]

At the time of the composition of *Carnaval*, Schumann was in love with Ernestine von Fricken, who came from Asch, and to whom the work was dedicated. Practically all the pieces use the four letters as a basis. In the "Sphinxs" from *Carnaval*, he uses the four letters enigmatically to represent himself and Ernestine von Fricken. In 1840 he writes:

The name of a little town, where a musical friend lived, contained actual letters of the scale, which also happen to be in my name; so one of those pastimes came about, which, after Bach's example, was no longer new. One piece after the other was finished, and this [occurred] exactly at carnival time, 1835, . . . Later I gave titles to the pieces and called the collection *Carnaval*. Some of them may appeal to one person, and some to another; after all, the musical moods change too quickly to allow a whole audience to follow them, unless it wants to be startled every minute.[262]

The letters ASCH explain little concerning any deeper musical meaning of *Carnaval*. As musical notes, they form the basis of a *soggetto cavato;* they provide a *cantus firmus* for many of the pieces; and are the kernel for a network of variations built on A flat, E flat, C, B and A flat, C, B.

Carnaval did not have a spontaneous development, but rather evolved through a process of elimination; furthermore, no evidence exists in Schumann's writings of an attempt to correlate the pieces with a definite story. Although Schumann adds titles later, it may be assumed that the idea of a program previously occurred to him. But if he had begun with a definite story which he intended to illustrate through music, he probably would have used the literary source as a starting point. As it was, he kept only those pieces which he believed were, first of all, musically appropriate. The title for the collection was selected at a later date. He had originally considered the name *Spreu* (chaff), and in 1836, two years after the pieces were composed, they were mentioned in the *Neue Zeitschrift für Musik*, April 22, 1836 as *Fasching. Schwänke auf vier Noten f. Pfte. von Florestan. Opus 12.*

With *Kinderszenen*, Schumann moves a step farther away from the romantic conception of a union of the arts. The pieces have captions, but they are not related to a definite story. The collection is held together by the complementary and contrasting moods which it depicts, as well as musically through tonalities.

In *Kinderszenen*, the meaning Schumann attaches to titles is clearly proclaimed in a dispute he had with the critic Rellstab. The latter labeled the pieces "snapshots of childlife", which is exactly the opposite of what Schumann intended.[263] In a letter to his counterpoint teacher, Heinrich Dorn, dated September 5, 1839, Schumann insists that the titles are only indicative of a general mood he wants to create.

Anything more inept and narrow-minded I have never easily come across, than what Rellstab has written about my *Kinderszenen*. He really thinks that I place a crying child before me and then search for tones accordingly. It is the other way around. However, I do not deny that while composing, some children's heads were hovering around me, but of course the titles originated afterwards and are, indeed nothing but delicate directions for execution and interpretation.[264]

Schumann thinks about his childhood when he writes the pieces; and because at the same time he was struggling with Wieck for Clara, it is not surprising to find him claiming that they contain thoughts of her.

The day before yesterday, I received your kind letter about *Kinderszenen*. How I reveled and dreamt, as I wrote them, and if you ask me, whether your thoughts about it are also mine, then I think with delight: Yes, they are. What I shyly poeticized perhaps reality will bring us. . . .[265]

A more direct connection between Clara's influence and the idea of representing childhood scenes is shown in the following quotation from a letter to her.

It was a reminiscence of your words, when you wrote me that I appear sometimes to you like a child—in short, I felt quite like [I did] in my childhood days, and then I wrote about thirty small quaint things, from which I have selected twelve and called them *Kinderszenen*. You will enjoy them, but you must completely forget yourself as a virtuoso.[266]

As with *Papillons* and *Carnaval*, *Kinderszenen* also evolved through a process of elimination. Although there is no definite story connecting the pieces contained in *Kinderszenen*, they do have captions. With *Kreisleriana*, Schumann abandons titles, and only loosely relates the work to literature. On the surface *Papillons* appears to be similar to *Kreisleriana*, but the relationship between words and music is much stronger in the earlier work.

The subject of *Kreisleriana* is Kapellmeister Kreisler, as portrayed in E. T. A. Hoffmann's *Phantasiestücke in Callott's Manier* (1814-1815). As Marcel Brion expresses it:

Kreisler too was a fictional character; indeed no living man was ever of such vivid intensity, was ever so compelling as this "mad musician *par excellence.*" For he was no mere musician: he was the incarnation of music itself and of romantic music at that. He was at once the most fantastic and the most human of all Hoffmann's creations, because created in his own image. The whole romantic music has recognized its reflection in Kreisler.[267]

On a broader level the piece can be considered as a reflection of Schumann's personality, because the above description is appropriate for his own interpretation of Kreisler. In writing to Simonin de Sire, March 15, 1835, Schumann claims, "the title is intelligible only to Germans. Kreisler is a figure created by E. T. A. Hoffmann, an eccentric, wild, spirited Kapellmeister. There is much about him you will like." [268]

Although the eight fantasies which comprise *Kreisleriana* were composed with Kapellmeister Kreisler as a focal point, they also contain thoughts of Clara's love. Clara is not connected directly to the music; she rather serves as an inspiration for it. This in no way negates Hoffmann's influence, but rather reinforces the idea of the pieces being a reflection of Schumann's personality, which is akin to Kreisler's.

But Clara, this music now in me, and always with beautiful melodies! Imagine, since my last letter I again have ready a whole book of new things. *Kreisleriana* I want to call it, in which you and a thought of you play the chief part, and I will dedicate it to you—yes, to you and to no one else—you will smile so graciously when you recognize yourself. My music now comes to me so wonderfully entwined despite all its simplicity, speaking so eloquently from the heart, and thus it also effects everyone for whom I play it, which I now do gladly and often! [269]

A truly wild love is to be found there in some movements, and your life and mine and many of your glances.[270]

With *Kreisleriana* Schumann moves even farther from the romantic conception of a direct union of words and music. Although titles are important to Schumann, as was shown with *Carnaval* and *Kinderszenen*, they are to serve as directional guideposts, indicating the general emotional mood Schumann wants to present. Schumann intends to awaken in the listener a set of experiences excited by the general emotion which is depicted by the music. The particular reaction of each listener will differ according to his individual personality.

179

CHAPTER VII

CONCLUSION

In this book, we have attempted to present systematically Schumann's aesthetics. We have not tried to bring forth a new theory on Schumann, but rather to clarify issues which have been misconstrued by other writers or omitted from consideration. Previously, Schumann's aesthetics have been covered cursorily in biographies and scattered articles.

To facilitate an understanding of Schumann's mind, we examined the intellectual milieu in which Schumann worked. It was found that he read or was at least affected by several of the great romantic poets and philosophers, namely, Jean Paul, Wackenroder, Tieck, Thibaut, E. T. A. Hoffmann, Hegel, and Schopenhauer. His writings mention his indebtedness to some of them, and his thinking shows their influence in many ways. The piano music written between 1830-1840 reflects particularly the romantic side of his aesthetic concepts.

With these ideas in mind, we investigated Schumann's criticism. Romantic critics such as Hazlitt, F. Schlegel, A. Schlegel, Wackenroder, and Novalis influenced Schumann's critical viewpoint. We found that while Schumann believes in the subjective nature of criticism, he still recognizes the need for objective standards. He established both the *Davidsbund* and the *Neue Zeitschrift für Musik* for the extension of his ideas.

Schumann's artistic development, it has been shown, is closely associated with his aesthetic and critical maturation. As a young man, Schumann is an enthusiastic idealist who wants to see his principles realized and propagated; much of his adverse criticism on music arises from a deep-seated sense of disappointment with the world and specifically, with existing musical conditions. His early subjective viewpoint gradually becomes more objective. For example, as he begins to study counterpoint and the works of Bach, he sacrifices a portion of the earlier subjectivity which is associated with his earlier piano compositions of the 1830s. Schumann becomes more conscious of technique, and loses some of his former spontaneity. Although Schumann believes in the importance of improvisation and fantasy, he nevertheless takes into account the necessity for careful thought and revision.

During Schumann's most romantic period, from about 1830-1840, the romantic movement itself reached its height. During these years, as has been shown, Schumann extolls the immediate, the first expression. After 1840, Schumann begins to become more and more classical as does the world of art in general. In retrospect the change toward classicism appears to have been somewhat foreign to Schumann; the studied classic pieces and the second editions of some of his earlier works, rather than being the outpouring of the inspiration of the Creative Spirit, are calculated and sonorous, with, it seems, some concessions made to the fingers and the concert hall.

Although there is a general move toward classicism between 1830-1840, there is some evidence of reversion to romanticism. For example, in *Faschingsschwank aus Wien,* written in 1839, he returns to the festive spirit of *Carnaval.* This may be interpreted as a foreshadowing of the outburst of romanticism, which occurred in 1840, when Schumann devotes himself almost exclusively to the composition of songs, a typically romantic form. After the songs of 1840-1841 Schumann concentrates on more classical forms, such as the symphony, concerto, string quartet, piano trio, oratorio and opera.

His piano music written after 1840 also points to a more classical bias, although a trend from a more romantic to a more classic composer cannot be seen in any unbroken chronological sequence. Schumann writes works which are quite romantic, for example *Waldszenen,* written in 1849. The individual pieces contained within *Waldszenen* are linked together tonally, and are united by a single theme. Each piece has a title which connotes a forest scene. Secondly, after 1840 Schumann groups miniatures together which are unified more by musical than extramusical means, for example, *Albumblätter,* Opus 124, which were written between 1832-1845. Each piece has a title, and often they are very romantic, but there is no attempt to relate them to one idea or mood. The *Phantasiestücke,* Opus 111, which were written in 1851, are even more classical. The work has the same romantic title as Opus 12—*Phantasiestücke,* but the individual pieces contained in the *Phantasiestücke,* Opus 111, have no titles, whereas the ones in Opus 12 all bear captions.

Schumann also employs more classical forms in his smaller piano pieces after 1840, for example, the *Vier Märsche* Opus 76, written in 1849, and the *Drei Klavier-Sonaten für die Jugend,* Opus 118, written in 1853. In his collection of smaller pieces, for example, *Album für die Jugend,* Schumann uses classical as well as baroque forms, such as the choral, sicilian, canon, fugue, and figured choral. Schumann's interest in the baroque extends to his writing *Studien für den Pedal Flügel,* Opus 56, which were written in 1845 and employ canonic devices, and *Vier Fugen,* Opus 72, which date from the same year.

Furthermore, Schumann writes larger works for piano which use classical forms, for example, the *Andante mit Variationen,* Opus 46, for two pianos and the *Concerto,* Opus 54. After 1840 Schumann becomes more interested in composing chamber music and the piano plays a major role in this genre. He writes a piano quintet, a piano quartet, three piano trios, and two violin sonatas.

Nevertheless, the trend from romanticism to classicism which took place in Schumann's development, must be understood as occurring within a general romantic framework. In his music Schumann tries to capture the whole of experience. He is affected by extra-musical influences, especially by literature. This was seen in his conception of programmatic music, in which Schumann is aware of the relationship between literature and music, and deliberately works to achieve effects based on it. However, despite his interest in the philosophic and literary, he never allows theory to dominate the essential musical nature of his art. Schumann is basically a romantic composer, and his attempt to incorporate classic ideas may be seen as a desire to remain part of both schools. Following the Hegelian dialectic he tries to create a synthesis of romanticism and classicism.

Romanticism did not in fact devour its parent, rationalism or classicism. The eighteenth century lingered on, and paradoxically it is often the eighteenth-century survivals into the nineteenth that are most frequently attacked as the distinctive traits of Romanticism. By the time that Romanticism had purged itself of sentimentality, self-pity, and grandiloquence, and had thus found its unique character, it appears to some observers unrecognizable or "chastened," which is equivalent to saying that the ungainliness of adolescence is the true figure of the man.[271]

NOTES *

1. For a representative list of the biographies and articles written about Schumann, see Bibliography.
2. Georg Hegel, *Science of Logic*, translated by W. H. Johnston and L. G. Struthers (New York: Macmillan, 1929), Vol. II, p. 484.
3. See Robert Schumann, *Gesammelte Schriften über Musik und Musiker*, edited by Paul Bekker (Berlin: Wegweiser-Verlag, 1922), p. 33. The term "philosopher" is used here to mean one who presents, constructs and develops an organized, systematic and structured body of material. Bekker describes Schumann as not being a logician, [*Logiker*], i.e., one who arranges his thinking in an organized form.
Schumann was no logician, neither in terms of thought nor emotion. This characteristic, closely connected with the nature of his talent, led him to the sketch, the small aphoristic form, permitted him the more extensive ones only in rhapsodic terms, but forbade him all wide-ranging organically closed structures.

4. Mosco Carner, "The Orchestral Music," in *Schumann: A Symposium*, edited by Gerald Abraham (London: Oxford University Press, 1952), p. 187, comments that the first allegro of Beethoven's *Eroica* symphony had a strong influence on Schumann's Symphony in G minor. See Carner, *op. cit.*, pp. 187-190, for a more complete analysis of this point.
5. Jacques Barzun, *Berlioz and the Romantic Century* (Boston: Little, Brown and Co., 1950), Vol. I, p. 386.
6. J. H. Elliot, *Berlioz* (London: J. M. Dent & Sons, Ltd., 1938), p. 116.
Barzun disagrees with this view of Berlioz although he is convinced of the general cyclical movement. Berlioz "transcended as well as embodied his time, and his greatness for us lies precisely in this, that he gives us text and commentary in one living shape: at all key points his life and art furnish an explicit critique of his age. . . . He refuses to fit into any familiar category, . . ." (Jacques Barzun, *Berlioz and the Romantic Century* [Boston: Little, Brown and Co., 1950], Vol. I, p. 8.)

7. René Wellek, *A History of Modern Criticism: 1750-1950* (New Haven: Yale University Press, 1955), Vol. I, p. 124.
8. Jacob Burckhardt, *The Civilization of the Renaissance in Italy*, translated by G. C. Middlemore (London: George G. Harrap & Co., 1929), p. 143.
In the Middle Ages both sides of human consciousness—that which

*Unless otherwise indicated, all translations from the German were made by the author.

was turned within as that which was turned without—lay dreaming or half awake beneath a common veil. The veil was woven of faith, illusion, and childish prepossession, through which the world and history were seen clad in strange hues. Man was conscious of himself only as member of a race, people, party, family, or corporation—only through some general category. In Italy this veil first melted into air; an *objective* treatment and consideration of the State and of all the things of this world became possible. The *subjective* side at the same time asserted itself with corresponding emphasis; man became a spiritual *individual,* and recognized himself as such.

9. Johann Gottfried Herder, *Sämtliche Werke,* edited by B. Suphan, C. Redlich *et. al.,* 33 vols. (Berlin: Weidmann, 1877-1913), Vol. XVIII, p. 131, translated and quoted in René Wellek, *A History of Modern Criticism: 1750-1950* (New Haven: Yale University Press, 1955), Vol. I, p. 184.

10. Johann Gottfried Herder, quoted in Paul Moos, *Die Philosophie der musik* (Berlin: Schuster und Loeffler, 1922), p. 42.

11. Johann Gottfried Herder, quoted in Hermann Pfrogner, *Musik, Geschichte ihrer Deutung* (Freiburg: K. Alber, 1954), p. 262.

12. Robert Schumann, quoted in and translated by Wilhelm Joseph von Wasielewski, *Life of Robert Schumann* (Boston: Oliver Ditson, 1871), p. 31.

13. René Wellek, *A History of Modern Criticism: 1750-1950* (New Haven: Yale University Press, 1955), Vol. II, p. 101.

14. Jean Paul, quoted in Paul Moos, *Die Philosophie der Musik* (Berlin: Schuster und Loeffler, 1922), pp. 114-115.

15. Jean Paul, quoted in Hans Kötz, *Der Einfluss Jean Pauls auf Robert Schumann* (Weimar: H. Böhlau Nachfolger, 1933), p. 95.

16. *Ibid.*

17. Jean Paul, quoted in Ernst Glöckner, *Studien zur romantischen Psychologie der Musik* (München: Steinicke, 1909), p. 20.

18. Jean Paul's idea on the place of the genius in society has its musical reflection, for example, in the piece "Der Dichter spricht", where the genius is elevated above society. For Schumann's ideas on the role of the genius, see Chapter III.

19. Jean Paul, *Die Vorschule der Ästhetik* (Weimar: Hermann Böhlau, 1935), pp. 23-24; p. 34.

20. *Ibid.*, p. 55.

21. *Ibid.*, p. 49.

22. *Ibid.*, p. 37.

23. *Ibid.*, p. 40.

24. *Ibid.*, p. 49.

25. Jean Paul, quoted in Hans Kötz, *Der Einfluss Jean Pauls auf Robert Schumann* (Weimar: H. Böhlau Nachfolger, 1933), pp. 41-42.

26. Francisco D'Ollanda, *Three Dialogues,* (Rome, 1538), translated and quoted in Charles Holroyd, *Michael Angelo Buonarroti* (London: Duckworth & Co., 1903), p. 296.
". . . I sometimes set myself thinking and imagining that I find

amongst men but one single art or science, and that is drawing or painting, all others being members proceeding therefrom; for if you carefully consider all that is being done in this life you will find that each person is, without knowing it, painting this world, creating and producing new forms and figures here, in dress and the various garbs, in building and occupying spaces with painted buildings and houses, in cultivating the fields and ploughing the land into pictures and sketches, in navigating the seas with sails, in fighting and dividing the spoil, and finally in the 'firmamentos' and burials and in all other operations, movements and actions."

27. Wilhelm Heinrich Wackenroder and Ludwig Tieck, quoted in Paul Moos, *Moderne Musikästhetik in Deutschland* (Leipzig: H. Seemann Nachfolger, 1902), p. 63.

28. Wilhelm Heinrich Wackenroder and Ludwig Tieck, quoted in Hermann Pfrogner, *Musik, Geschichte ihrer Deutung* (Freiburg: K. Alber, 1954), p. 259.

29. Wilhelm Heinrich Wackenroder and Ludwig Tieck, quoted in Felix M. Gatz, *Musikästhetik in ihren Hauptrichtungen* (Stuttgart: F. Enke, 1929), p. 334.

30. Wilhelm Heinrich Wackenroder and Ludwig Tieck, quoted in Herbert Schulze, *Zur Frage der Ästhetischen Anschauungen Robert Schumanns* (Dresden: MS, 1954), p. 9.

31. René Wellek, *A History of Modern Criticism: 1750-1950* (New Haven: Yale University Press, 1955), Vol. II, p. 91.

32. Anton Friedrich Thibaut, *Ueber Reinheit der Tonkunst* (Heidelberg: Mohr, 1875), p. 9.

33. Anton Friedrich Thibaut, quoted in Herbert Schulze, *Zur Frage der Ästhetischen Anschauungen Robert Schumanns* (Dresden: MS, 1954), pp. 52-53.

34. Anton Friedrich Thibaut, *Ueber Reinheit der Tonkunst* (Heidelberg: Mohr, 1875), pp. 60-61.

35. *Ibid.*, p. 110.

36. *Ibid.*, p. 168.

37. *Ibid.*, pp. 124-125.

38. *Ibid.*, pp. 45-46.

39. *Ibid.*, p. 92.

40. E. T. A. Hoffmann, quoted in Paul Moos, *Die Philosophie der Musik* (Berlin: Schuster und Loeffler, 1922), p. 123.

41. E. T. A. Hoffmann, quoted in Felix M. Gatz, *Musikästhetik in ihren Hauptrichtungen* (Stuttgart: Enke, 1929), p. 361.

42. E. T. A. Hoffmann, quoted in Paul Moos, *Die Philosophie der Musik* (Berlin: Schuster und Loeffler, 1922), p. 123.

43. Georg Hegel, *Vorlesungen über die Ästhetik in Sämtliche Werke*, edited by Hermann Glöckner (Stuttgart: Frommann, 1928), Vol. I, p. 68, translated and quoted in René Wellek, *A History of Modern Criticism: 1750-1950* (New Haven: Yale University Press, 1955), Vol. II, p. 320.

44. Georg Hegel, quoted in Paul Moos, *Moderne Musikästhetik in Deutschland* (Leipzig: H. Seemann Nachfolger, 1902), p. 23.

45. Georg Hegel, quoted in Kurt Huber, *Musikästhetik* (Stuttgart: Ettal, Buch-Kunst-Verlag, 1954), p. 63.

46. Georg Hegel, quoted in Hermann Pfrogner, *Musik, Geschichte ihrer Deutung* (Freiburg: K. Alber, 1954), p. 276.

47. Georg Hegel, quoted in Paul Moos, *Die Philosophie der Musik* (Berlin: Schuster und Loeffler, 1922), p. 140.

48. Georg Hegel, *ibid.*, p. 139.

49. Georg Hegel, quoted in Hanns Frömbgen-Essen, "Hegel und die musikalische Romantik—Die Erhellung der Musik durch die Philosophie," *Die Musik*, XXI (1929), 657.

50. Arthur Schopenhauer, *Sämtliche Werke*, edited by A. Hübscher (Leipzig: F. A. Brockhaus, 1937), Vol. II, p. 217, translated by R. B. Haldane and J. Kemp, *The World as Will and Idea*, Vol. I, p. 239, quoted in René Wellek, *A History of Modern Criticism: 1750-1950* (New Haven: Yale University Press, 1955), Vol. II, p. 311.

51. René Wellek, *A History of Modern Criticism: 1750-1950* (New Haven: Yale University Press, 1955), Vol. II, p. 311.

52. Arthur Schopenhauer, quoted in Paul Moos, *Die Philosophie der Musik* (Berlin: Schuster und Loeffler, 1922), p. 153.

53. Arthur Schopenhauer, quoted in Hermann Pfrogner, *Musik, Geschichte ihrer Deutung* (Freiburg: K. Alber, 1954), p. 282.

54. Arthur Schopenhauer, quoted in Paul Moos, *Moderne Musikästhetik in Deutschland* (Leipzig: H. Seemann Nachfolger, 1902), p. 42.

55. Robert Schumann, quoted in Hans Kötz, *Der Einfluss Jean Pauls auf Robert Schumann* (Weimar: H. Böhlau Nachfolger, 1933), p. 29.

56. Robert Schumann, *Gesammelte Schriften über Musik und Musiker*, edited by Paul Bekker (Berlin: Wegweiser-Verlag, 1922), p. 33.

57. Robert Schumann, quoted in Wolfgang Boetticher, *Robert Schumann in seinen Schriften und Briefen* (Berlin: Hahnefeld, 1942), p. 10.

58. Robert Schumann, quoted in Wolfgang Boetticher, *Robert Schumann: Einführung in Persönlichkeit und Werk* (Berlin: Hahnefeld, 1941), pp. 114-115. This quotation reveals the influence of Jean Paul, especially in the concept of music as the spiritual language of emotion [*Geistersprache des Gefühls*].

59. Robert Schumann, quoted in Karl Heinrich Wörner, *Robert Schumann* (Zürich: Atlantis, 1949), p. 33.

60. Robert Schumann, quoted in Arnold Schmitz, "Anfänge der Ästhetik Robert Schumanns," *Zeitschrift für Musikwissenschaft*, II, No. 9 (June, 1920), 538.

61. Robert Schumann, quoted in F. Gustav Jansen, "Aus Robert Schumanns Schulzeit," *Die Musik*, V, No. 20 (1905-1906), 92.

62. Robert Schumann, *Gesammelte Schriften über Musik und Musiker* (Leipzig: Breitkopf und Härtel, 1914), Vol. II, p. 276.

63. Robert Schumann, quoted in Wolfgang Boetticher, *Robert*

Schumann: *Einführung in Persönlichkeit und Werk* (Berlin: Hahnefeld, 1941), p. 338.

64. Robert Schumann, *Gesammelte Schriften über Musik und Musiker* (Leipzig: Breitkopf und Härtel, 1914), Vol. II, p. 115.

65. *Ibid.*, Vol. I, p. 26.

66. *Ibid.*, Vol. II, p. 175.

67. Robert Schumann, quoted in Hans Kötz, *Der Einfluss Jean Pauls auf Robert Schumann* (Weimar: H. Böhlau Nachfolger, 1933), p. 14.

68. Robert Schumann, quoted in Karl Heinrich Wörner, *Robert Schumann* (Zürich: Atlantis, 1949), pp. 25-26.

69. Robert Schumann, *Gesammelte Schriften über Musik und Musiker* (Leipzig: Breitkopf und Härtel, 1914), Vol. II, pp. 184-185.

70. For example, William Wordsworth, the English romantic poet, describes the "overflow of feelings" in the following terms.
. . . "it takes its origin from emotion recollected in tranquillity; the emotion is contemplated till, by a species of reaction, the tranquillity gradually disappears, and an emotion, kindred to that which was before the subject of contemplation, is gradually produced, and does itself actually exist in the mind." (William Wordsworth, *Wordsworth's Literary Criticism*, edited by N. C. Smith [London, Oxford, 1905], pp. 34-35, quoted in René Wellek, *A History of Modern Criticism: 1750-1950* [New Haven: Yale University Press, 1955], Vol. II, p. 139.) France exhibits a similar current of thought in the writing of Diderot, who regards emotion as something extraordinary. "Clarity is all right for convincing: . . . Clarity of whatever kind damages enthusiasm. Poets, speak incessantly of eternity, infinitude, immensity, time, space, divinity. . . . Be dark!" "The vaguer is expression in the arts, the more is imagination at ease." (Dennis Diderot, *Oeuvres*, edited by J. Assézat and M. Tourneux, 20 vols. [Paris: Garnier Frères, 1875-1879], Vol. XI, p. 147, and Vol. X, p. 352, translated and cited in René Wellek, *A History of Modern Criticism: 1750-1950*, Vol. I, p. 51.

71. Robert Schumann, *Jugendbriefe* (Leipzig: Breitkopf und Härtel, 1886), p. 136.

72. Robert Schumann, quoted in Wolfgang Boetticher, *Robert Schumann: Einführung in Persönlichkeit und Werk* (Berlin: Hahnefeld, 1941), p. 109.

73. *Ibid.*, p. 109.

74. *Ibid.*, p. 110.

75. Robert Schumann, *Gesemmelte Schriften über Musik und Musiker* (Leipzig: Breitkopf und Härtel, 1914), Vol. I, p. 25.

76. Robert Schumann, quoted in Wolfgang Boetticher, *Robert Schumann: Einführung in Persönlichkeit und Werk* (Berlin: Hahnefeld, 1941), p. 111.

77. Robert Schumann, quoted in Wolfgang Boetticher, "Robert Schumann in seinen Beziehungen zu Johannes Brahms," *Die Musik*, XXIX (1937), 553.

78. Robert Schumann, *Gesammelte Schriften über Musik und Musiker* (Leipzig: Breitkopf und Härtel, 1914), Vol. I, p. 106.

79. Robert Schumann, quoted in Hans Kötz, *Der Einfluss Jean Pauls auf Robert Schumann* (Weimar: H. Böhlau Nachfolger, 1933), p. 39.

80. Robert Schumann, *Gesammelte Schriften über Musik und Musiker* (Leipzig: Breitkopf und Härtel, 1914), Vol. I, p. 355.

81. Robert Schumann, quoted in Karl Heinrich Wörner, *Robert Schumann* (Zürich: Atlantis, 1949), p. 83.

82. *Ibid.*

83. Robert Schumann, *Gesammelte Schriften über Musik und Musiker* (Leipzig: Breitkopf und Härtel, 1914), Vol. I, p. 167.

84. Robert Schumann, quoted in Wolfgang Boetticher, *Robert Schumann: Einführung in Persönlichkeit und Werk* (Berlin: Hahnefeld, 1941), p. 295.

85. Robert Schumann, *Robert Schumanns Briefe*, edited by F. Gustav Jansen (Leipzig: Breitkopf und Härtel, 1904), p. 312.

86. For instance, René Wellek interprets Marmontel's view of the genius as follows, "Genius is merely the inventive faculty, while the actual composition of a work of art is due to talent and taste and to the observance of the rules." (René Wellek, *A History of Modern Criticism: 1750-1950* [New Haven: Yale University Press, 1955], Vol. I, pp. 65-66). Perhaps this differentiation is stated best by Coleridge, the English romantic poet and literary critic. René Wellek interprets his thought as follows:
Genius and imagination in the poet are distinguished from corresponding lower faculties, talent and fancy. These are not opposites in the sense that genius excludes talent, or imagination excludes fancy. Rather, genius needs talent and imagination needs fancy. Still, they are distinct and widely different faculties. Genius and imagination are unifying, reconciling: they belong to the level of Coleridge's holistic and dialectical thought, while talent and fancy are only combinatory and thus mechanistic, associationist. Genius is a gift, talent is manufactured; genius is creative, talent mechanical.
(René Wellek, *A History of Modern Criticism: 1750-1950* [New Haven: Yale University Press, 1955], Vol. II, p. 164.

87. Robert Schumann, *Gesammelte Schriften über Musik und Musiker* (Leipzig: Breitkopf und Härtel, 1914), Vol. I, p. 420.

88. *Ibid.*, p. 295.

89. *Ibid.*, Vol. II, p. 8.

90. Robert Schumann, quoted in Wolfgang Boetticher, *Robert Schumann in seinen Schriften und Briefen* (Berlin: Hahnefeld, 1942), p. 68.

91. Robert Schumann, *Gesammelte Schriften über Musik und Musiker* (Leipzig: Breitkopf und Härtel, 1914), Vol. II, p. 355.

92. Robert Schumann, *Jugendbriefe* (Leipzig: Breitkopf und Härtel, 1886), p. 30.

93. Robert Schumann, quoted in Wolfgang Boetticher, *Robert*

Schumann in seinen Schriften und Briefen (Berlin: Hahnefeld, 1942), p. 32.

94. Robert Schumann, quoted in Wolfgang Boetticher, *Robert Schumann in seinen Schriften und Briefen* (Berlin: Hahnefeld, 1942), p. 440.

95. Michel de Montaigne, "Of Solitariness," *The Essays*, translated by John Florio (New York & London: The Knickerbocker Press, 1907), p. 216.

Now since we undertake to live solitary, and without company, let us cause our contentment to depend of ourselves: let us shake off all bonds that tie us unto others: gain we that victory over us, that in good earnest we may live solitary, and therein live at our ease.

96. Robert Schumann, *Gesammelte Schriften über Musik und Musiker* (Leipzig: Breitkopf und Härtel, 1914), Vol. II, p. 188.

97. Robert Schumann, quoted in Hermann Erler, *Robert Schumanns Leben und Werke aus seinen Briefen geschildert* (Leipzig: Ries und Erler, 1887), Vol. I, p. 3.

98. Robert Schumann, *Jugendbriefe* (Leipzig: Breitkopf und Härtel, 1886), p. 298.

99. Robert Schumann, *Gesammelte Schriften über Musik und Musiker* (Leipzig: Breitkopf und Härtel, 1914), Vol. I, p. 330.

100. William Hazlitt, *Complete Works*, edited by P. P. Howe (London: Dent, 1930), Vol. V, p. 175, as quoted in René Wellek, *A History of Modern Criticism: 1750-1950* (New Haven: Yale University Press, 1955), Vol. II, p. 195.

101. Ugo Foscolo, "Review," *Edinburgh Review*, 29 (1818), 460; as cited and translated in René Wellek, *op. cit.*, Vol. II, p. 268.

102. Gotthold Lessing, *Werke*, edited by Franz Bornmüller (Leipzig: Bibliographisches Institut, 1884), Vol. IV, p. 422; as cited and translated in René Wellek, *op. cit.*, Vol. I, p. 170.

103. Johann Wolfgang von Goethe, *Werke*, edited by Eduard von der Hellen (Stuttgart: J. G. Cotta Nachfolger, 1902-07), Vol. 17, p. 251; as cited in René Wellek, *op. cit.*, Vol. I, p. 205.

104. *Ibid.*, Vol. 37, pp. 279-280; as cited and translated in René Wellek, *op. cit.*, Vol. I, p. 224.

105. Friedrich Schlegel, quoted in Jakob Minor, *Friedrich Schlegel 1794-1802: seine prosaischen Jugendschriften* (Vienna: Konegen, 1882), Vol. I, p. 309; as cited in René Wellek, *op. cit.*, Vol. II, p. 10.

106. Friedrich Schlegel, "Introduction," *Lessings Geist aus seinen Schriften* (Leipzig: Hinrichs, 1804), Vol. I, pp. 40-41; as cited in René Wellek, *op. cit.*, Vol. II, p. 9.

107. Friedrich Schlegel, *Neue Philosophische Schriften* (Frankfurt: Josef Körner, 1935), p. 382; as cited in René Wellek, *op. cit.*, Vol. II, p. 9.

108. August Schlegel, *Über dramatische Kunst und Literatur* (Heidelberg: Mohr, 1817), Vol. I, pp. 5-6; as cited in René Wellek, *op. cit.*, Vol. II, p. 38.

189

109. René Wellek, *A History of Modern Criticism: 1750-1950* (New Haven: Yale University Press, 1955), Vol. II, pp. 48-49.

110. Wilhelm Wackenroder, *Werke und Briefe* (Berlin: L. Schneider, 1938), p. 222; as cited in René Wellek, *op. cit.*, Vol. II, p. 90.

111. Novalis, *Gesammelte Werke*, ed. by Carl Seelig (Zürich: Atlantis, 1945), Vol. II, p. 192; as cited in René Wellek, *op. cit.*, Vol. II, pp. 86-87.

112. Robert Schumann, quoted in F. Gustav Jansen, *Die Davidsbündler* (Leipzig: Breitkopf und Härtel, 1883), p. 17.

113. Robert Schumann, quoted in Wolfgang Boetticher, *Robert Schumann in seinen Schriften und Briefen* (Berlin: Hahnefeld, 1942), p. 87.

114. Robert Schumann, *Gesammelte Schriften über Musik und Musiker* (Leipzig: Breitkopf und Härtel, 1914), Vol. I, p. 422.

115. *Ibid.*, Vol. II, p. 72.

116. Robert Schumann, *Robert Schumanns Briefe*, edited by F. Gustav Jansen (Leipzig: Breitkopf und Härtel, 1904), p. 482.

117. Robert Schumann, quoted in Hermann Erler, *Robert Schumanns Leben und Werke aus seinen Briefen geschildert* (Leipzig: Ries und Erler, 1887), Vol. II, p. 179.

118. Robert Schumann, *Robert Schumanns Briefe*, edited by F. Gustav Jansen (Leipzig: Breitkopf und Härtel, 1904), pp. 292-293.

119. Robert Schumann, *Gesammelte Schriften über Musik und Musiker* (Leipzig: Breitkopf und Härtel, 1914), Vol. I, p. 492.

120. *Ibid.*, p. 52.

121. Robert Schumann, quoted in F. Gustav Jansen, *Die Davidsbündler* (Leipzig: Breitkopf und Härtel, 1883), p. 33.

122. Robert Schumann, quoted in Wolfgang Boetticher, *Robert Schumann in seinen Schriften und Briefen* (Berlin: Hahnefeld, 1942), p. 74.

123. Robert Schumann, quoted in F. Gustav Jansen, *Die Davidsbündler* (Leipzig: Breitkopf und Härtel, 1883), p. 14.

124. Robert Schumann, *Gesammelte Schriften über Musik und Musiker* (Leipzig: Breitkopf und Härtel, 1914), Vol. II, p. 267.

125. Robert Schumann, quoted in Karl Heinrich Wörner, *Robert Schumann* (Zürich: Atlantis, 1949), p. 78.

126. Robert Schumann quoted in Wolfgang Boetticher, *Robert Schumann in seinen Schriften und Briefen* (Berlin: Hahnefeld, 1942), p. 67.

127. Robert Schumann, quoted in Arnold Schmitz, "Die Ästhetischen Anschauungen Robert Schumanns in ihren Beziehungen zur Romantischen Literatur," *Zeitschrift für Musikwissenschaft*, III (1920-1921), 117-118.

128. Robert Schumann, *Robert Schumanns Briefe*, edited by F. Gustav Jansen (Leipzig: Breitkopf und Härtel, 1904), p. 153.

129. Robert Schumann, *Gesammelte Schriften über Musik und Musiker* (Leipzig: Breitkopf und Härtel, 1914), Vol. I, p. 284.

130. Robert Schumann, quoted in F. Gustav Jansen, *Die Davidsbündler* (Leipzig: Breitkopf und Härtel, 1883), pp. 24-25.

131. Robert Schumann, *Gesammelte Schriften über Musik und Musiker* (Leipzig: Breitkopf und Härtel, 1914), Vol. I, p. 17.

132. *Ibid.*, Vol. I, p. 337.

133. *Ibid.*, Vol. II, pp. 23-24.

134. *Ibid.*, Vol. I, p. 75.

135. Robert Schumann, *Robert Schumanns Briefe*, edited by F. Gustav Jansen (Leipzig: Breitkopf und Härtel, 1904), p. 256.

136. Robert Schumann, *Gesammelte Schriften über Musik und Musiker* (Leipzig: Breitkopf und Härtel, 1914), Vol. I, pp. 323-324.

137. Robert Schumann, quoted in F. Gustav Jansen, *Die Davidsbündler* (Leipzig: Breitkopf und Härtel, 1883), pp. 5-6.

138. Robert Schumann, quoted in Karl Heinrich Wörner, *Robert Schumann* (Zürich: Atlantis, 1949), pp. 79-80.

139. See Chapter V for a further discussion of Schumann's use of folkmusic.

140. Robert Schumann, *Gesammelte Schriften über Musik und Musiker* (Leipzig: Breitkopf und Härtel, 1914), Vol. I, pp. 462-463.

141. *Ibid.*, Vol. II, p. 213.

142. Robert Schumann, *Robert Schumanns Briefe*, edited by F. Gustav Jansen (Leipzig: Breitkopf und Härtel, 1904), p. 405.

143. Robert Schumann, *Gesammelte Schriften über Musik und Musiker* (Leipzig: Breitkopf und Härtel, 1914), Vol. I, p. 386.

144. *Ibid.*, Vol. II, pp. 88-89.

145. *Ibid.*, Vol. I, p. 128.

146. *Ibid.*, Vol. II, p. 250.

147. *Ibid.*, p. 91.

148. Robert Schumann, quoted in F. Gustav Jansen, *Die Davidsbündler* (Leipzig: Breitkopf und Härtel, 1883), p. 17.

149. Robert Schumann, *Robert Schumanns Briefe*, edited by F. Gustav Jansen (Leipzig: Breitkopf und Härtel, 1904), p. 285.

150. *Ibid.*, p. 78.

151. Robert Schumann, quoted in F. Gustav Jansen, *Die Davidsbündler* (Leipzig: Breitkopf und Härtel, 1883), pp. 36-37.

152. Robert Schumann, quoted in Gustav Wustmann, "Zur Entstehungsgeschichte der Schumannschen Zeitschrift für Musik," *Zeitschrift der Internationalen Musikgesellschaft*, VIII (1907), 397.

153. *Ibid.*

154. *Ibid.*, pp. 397-398.

155. William Shakespeare, *Henry VIII*, prologue, lines 13-17.

156. Robert Schumann, quoted in Hermann Erler, *Robert Schumanns Leben und Werke aus seinen Briefen geschildert* (Leipzig: Ries und Erler, 1887), Vol. I, p. 43. Original can be found in Example 8, p. 63.

157. F. Pessenlehner, "Robert Schumann und die Neue Zeitschrift für Musik," *Neue Zeitschrift für Musik* (1933), 18.

158. Robert Schumann, *Gesammelte Schriften über Musik und Musiker* (Leipzig: Breitkopf und Härtel, 1914), Vol. II, p. 330.

159. William Shakespeare, *A Midsummer Night's Dream*, Act 5, Scene 1, lines 16-17.

160. Robert Schumann, *Gesammelte Schriften über Musik und*

Musiker (Leipzig: Breitkopf und Härtel, 1914), Vol. II, pp. 129-130.
161. Faust contemplating the sign of the [*Makrokosmos*].
Wie alles sich zum Ganzen webt,
Eins in dem andern wirkt und lebt!
Wie Himmelskräfte auf und nieder steigen
Und sich die goldnen Eimer reichen!

How each the Whole its substance gives,
Each in the other works and lives!
See heavenly forces rising and descending,
Their golden urns reciprocally lending!
(Goethe, *Faust*, Part One, lines 247ff., Translation by Bayard Taylor).

162. Robert Schumann, *Gesammelte Schriften über Musik und Musiker* (Leipzig: Breitkopf und Härtel, 1914), Vol. I, p. 139.
163. Robert Schumann, quoted in Hans Kötz, *Der Einfluss Jean Pauls auf Robert Schumann* (Weimar: H. Böhlau Nachfolger, 1933), pp. 40-41.
164. Robert Schumann, quoted in Herbert Schulze, *Zur Frage der Ästhetischen Anschauungen Robert Schumann* (Dresden: MS, 1954), p. 22.
165. Robert Schumann, *Robert Schumanns Briefe*, edited by F. Gustav Jansen (Leipzig: Breitkopf und Härtel, 1904), p. 280.
166. Robert Schumann, quoted in Berthold Litzmann, *Clara Schumann: Ein Künstlerleben* (Leipzig: Breitkopf und Härtel, 1905-1909), Vol. I, p. 274.
167. Robert Schumann, quoted in Gerald Abraham, *Schumann: A Symposium* (London: Oxford University Press, 1952), p. 127 (Printed as it appears in the source).
168. Robert Schumann, *Gesammelte Schriften über Musik und Musiker* (Leipzig: Breitkopf und Härtel, 1914), Vol. I, p. 409.
169. Robert Schumann, *Jugendbriefe* (Leipzig: Breitkopf und Härtel, 1886), p. 278.
170. Robert Schumann, *Gesammelte Schriften über Musik und Musiker* (Leipzig: Breitkopf und Härtel, 1914), Vol. I, p. 398.
171. *Ibid.*, Vol. II, p. 259.
172. *Ibid.*, p. 16.
173. *Ibid.*, p. 139.
174. Robert Schumann, quoted in Hans Joachim Moser & Eberhard Rebling, *Robert Schumann* (Leipzig: Breitkopf und Härtel, 1956), p. 71.
175. Robert Schumann, *Jugendbriefe* (Leipzig: Breitkopf und Härtel, 1886), p. 146.
176. *Ibid.*, p. 146.
177. Robert Schumann, quoted in Wolfgang Boetticher, *Robert Schumann in seinen Schriften und Briefen* (Berlin: Hahnefeld, 1942), pp. 395-396.
178. Robert Schumann, quoted in Wilhelm Joseph von Wasielewski, *Life of Schumann*, translated by A. L. Alger (Boston and New York: Oliver Ditson, 1876), p. 230.

179. Hermann Ludwig, Freiherr von der Pfordten, *Robert Schumann* (Leipzig: Quelle und Meyer, 1920), p. 58.

180. Robert Schumann, *Gesammelte Schriften über Musik und Musiker* (Leipzig: Breitkopf und Härtel, 1914), Vol. II, p. 11.

181. Robert Schumann, *Jugendbriefe* (Leipzig: Breitkopf und Härtel, 1886), p. 95.

182. Robert Schumann, quoted in Eugenie Schumann, *Robert Schumann: Ein Lebensbild meines Vaters* (Leipzig: Koehler und Amelang, 1931), p. 302.

183. J. A. Fuller-Maitland, *Schumann's Pianoforte Works* (London: Oxford University Press, 1927), p. 6.

184. Joan Chissel, *Schumann* (London: J. M. Dent, 1948), p. 113.

185. Robert Schumann, *Gesammelte Schriften über Musik und Musiker* (Leipzig: Breitkopf und Härtel, 1914), Vol. I, p. 373.

186. *Ibid.*, p. 59.

187. Ludwig van Beethoven, quoted and translated by J. W. N. Sullivan, *Beethoven: His Spiritual Development* (New York: Alfred Knopf, 1927), p. 50.

188. Ludwig van Beethoven, *The Letters of Beethoven*, edited and translated by Emily Anderson (New York: St. Martin's Press, 1961), Vol. II, p. 689.

189. Robert Schumann, quoted in Wolfgang Boetticher, *Robert Schumann: Einführung in Persönlichkeit und Werk* (Berlin: Hahnefeld, 1941), p. 206.

190. Robert Schumann, quoted in Berthold Litzmann, *Clara Schumann: Ein Künstlerleben* (Leipzig: Breitkopf und Härtel, 1905-1909), Vol. I, p. 310.

191. Robert Schumann, quoted in Wolfgang Boetticher, *Robert Schumann: Einführung in Persönlichkeit und Werk* (Berlin: Hahnefeld, 1941), p. 129.

192. Robert Schumann, *Gesammelte Schriften über Musik und Musiker* (Leipzig: Breitkopf und Härtel, 1914), Vol. I, p. 415.

193. *Ibid.*, Vol. II, p. 311.

194. Robert Schumann, *Gesammelte Schriften über Musik und Musiker* (Leipzig: Breitkopf und Härtel, 1914), Vol. I, pp. 183-184.

195. Robert Schumann, *Gesammelte Schriften über Musik und Musiker* (Leipzig: Breitkopf und Härtel, 1914), Vol. II, p. 11.

196. Robert Schumann, quoted in Wolfgang Boetticher, *Robert Schumann in seinen Schriften und Briefen* (Berlin: Hahnefeld, 1942), p. 254.

197. Robert Schumann, *Robert Schumanns Briefe*, edited by F. Gustav Jansen (Leipzig: Breitkopf und Härtel, 1904), p. 170.

198. Robert Schumann, *Gesammelte Schriften über Musik und Musiker* (Leipzig: Breitkopf und Härtel, 1914), Vol. I, p. 385.

199. Robert Schumann, quoted in Wolfgang Gertler, *Robert Schumann in seinen frühen Klavierwerken* (Leipzig: Druck von Radelli und Hille, 1931), p. 36.

200. Robert Schumann, *Gesammelte Schriften über Musik und Musiker* (Leipzig: Breitkopf und Härtel, 1914), Vol. I, p. 58.

201. Hermann von Helmholtz's classic work *Sensations of Tone* appeared in 1862, in which overtones were explained scientifically.

202. Donald N. Ferguson, *A History of Musical Thought* (New York and London: Appleton-Century-Crofts, Inc., 1948), p. 29.

203. Wolfgang Boetticher, *Einführung in Persönlichkeit und Werk* (Berlin: Hahnefeld, 1941), pp. 504-505.

204. Robert Schumann, quoted in Wolfgang Boetticher, *Robert Schumann: Einführung in Persönlichkeit und Werk* (Berlin: Hahnefeld, 1941), pp. 320-321.

205. Robert Schumann, *Gesammelte Schriften über Musik und Musiker* (Leipzig: Breitkopf und Härtel, 1914), Vol. II, p. 208.

206. Robert Schumann, *Gesammelte Schriften über Musik und Musiker* (Leipzig: Breitkopf und Härtel, 1914), Vol. I, p. 20.

207. Willi Apel, *Harvard Dictionary of Music* (Cambridge: Harvard University Press, 1947), p. 329.

208. Robert Schumann, quoted in Peter Sutermeister, *Robert Schumann* (Zürich: Ex-libris-Verlag, 1949), p. 80.

209. Victor Hugo, *Oeuvres complètes* (Paris: Hetzel et Quantin, 1881), Vol. 17, p. 16, also quoted in and translated by René Wellek, *A History of Modern Criticism: 1750–1950* (New Haven: Yale University Press, 1955), Vol. II, p. 255.

210. August Wilhelm Schlegel, *Vorlesungen über schöne Literatur und Kunst*, edited by Jakob Minor (Berlin: Behr, 1898), Vol. 2, p. 209, also quoted in and translated by René Wellek, *A History of Modern Criticism: 1750-1950* (New Haven: Yale University Press, 1955), Vol. II, p. 49.

211. Robert Schumann, *Robert Schumanns Briefe*, edited by F. Gustav Jansen (Leipzig: Breitkopf und Härtel, 1904), p. 137.

212. Robert Schumann, *Gesammelte Schriften über Musik und Musiker* (Leipzig: Breitkopf und Härtel, 1914), Vol. I, pp. 389-390.

213. *Ibid.*, Vol. I, p. 112.

214. *Ibid.*, Vol. II, pp. 64-65.

215. *Ibid.*, Vol. I, p. 73.

216. Robert Schumann, "Episode de la vie d'un Artiste," *Neue Zeitschrift für Musik*, III (August, 1835), 37. (See p. 195).

217. The following is a list of books analyzing Schumann's piano style. For further references, books and articles, consult the bibliography:

1. Marguerite d'Albert, *Robert Schumann, son oeuvre de piano* (Paris: Fischbasher, 1904).

2. Marcel Beaufils, *La Musique de Piano de Schumann* (Paris: Librarie Larousse, 1951).

3. Mosco Carner, *Studien zur Sonatenform bei Robert Schumann* (Wiener Diss.: MS, 1928).

4. Rosalie Goldenberg, *Der Klaviersatz bei Schumann* (Wiener Diss.: MS, 1931).

5. Werner Schwarz, *Robert Schumann und die Variation* (Kassel: Bärenreiter-Verlag, 1932).

6. M. Schweiger, *Die Harmonik in den Klavierwerken Schumanns* (Wiener Diss.: MS, 1931).

Robert Schumann, Neue Zeitschrift für Musik, August,
1835, p. 37.

Neue
Zeitschrift für Musik.

Im Vereine
mit mehren Künstlern und Kunstfreunden
herausgegeben unter Verantwortlichkeit von R. Schumann.

Dritter Band.   № 10.   Den 4. August 1835.

> Der seltne Mann will seltnes Vertrauen;
> Gebt ihm den Raum, das Ziel wird er sich setzen.
> Wallenstein.

Orchester.

Hector Berlioz,
Episode de la vie d'un Artiste etc.
(Fortsetzung.)

Berlioz kann kaum mit größerem Schmerze den Kopf eines schönen Mörders auseinander genommen haben, als ich seinen ersten Satz. Und hab' ich noch dazu meinen Lesern mit der Section etwas genützt? Aber ich wollte dreierlei damit: erstens denen, welchen die Symphonie gänzlich unbekannt ist, zeigen, wie wenig ihnen in der Musik durch eine zergliedernde Kritik überhaupt klar gemacht werden kann, denen, die sie oberflächlich durchgesehen und weil sie nicht gleich wußten, wo aus und ein, sie vielleicht bei Seite legten, in paar Höhenpuncte andeuten, endlich denen, die sie kennen, ohne sie anerkennen zu wollen, nachweisen, wie trotz der scheinbaren Formlosigkeit diesem Körper, in größeren Verhältnissen gemessen, eine wunderbare symmetrische Ordnung inwohnt, des inneren Zusammenhangs gar nicht zu erwähnen. Aber an dem Ungewohnten dieser neuen Form, des neuen Ausdrucks liegt wohl zum Theil der Grund zum unglücklichen Mißverständniß. Die Meisten haften beim ersten oder zweiten Anhören zu sehr an den Einzelnheiten und es verhält sich damit, wie mit dem Lesen einer schwierigen Handschrift, über deren Entzifferung einer, der sich bei jedem einzelnen Wort aufhält, ungleich mehr Zeit braucht, als der sie erst im Ganzen überfliegt, um Sinn und Absicht kennen zu lernen. Zudem, wie schon angedeutet, macht nichts so leicht Verdruß und Widerspruch als eine neue Form, die einen alten Namen trägt. Wollte z. B. Jemand etwas im Fünf-Viertel-Tact Geschriebenes einen Marsch, oder zwölf aneinander gereihte kleine Sätze eine Symphonie nennen, so nimmt er gewiß vorweg gegen sich ein, — indeß untersuche man immer, was an der Sache ist. Je sonderbarer und künstlicher also ein Werk augenscheinlich aussieht, je vorsichtiger sollte man urtheilen. Und gibt uns nicht die Erfahrung an Beethoven ein Beispiel, dessen, namentlich letzte Werke, sicherlich eben so ihrer eigenthümlichen Constructionen und Formen, in denen er so unerschöpflich erfand, wie des Geistes halber, den freilich Niemand läugnen konnte, im Anfang unverständlich gefunden wurden? Fassen wir jetzt, ohne uns durch kleine, allerdings oft scharf hervorspringende Ecken stören zu lassen, das ganze erste Allegro in weiteren Bogen zusammen, so stellt sich uns deutlich diese Form hervor:

```
                                        Erstes Thema.
                      Erstes Thema.   Mittelsätze mit einem   (G-Dur.)   Mittelsätze mit dem                Erstes Thema.
   Anfang.            (G-Dur.)        zweiten Thema.                     zweiten Thema.                     (G-Dur.)      Schluß.
   (G-Dur.)   .  .  .  .  .  .  .   (G-Dur, C-Moll.)  .  .  .  .  .  .  (C-Moll, G-Dur.)  .  .  .  .  .  .  .  .  .  .  .  (G-Dur.)

   der wir zum Vergleich die ältere Norm entgegenstellen:
                                             Mittelsatz
                      Zweites.              (A-Moll.)                    Erstes Thema.
   Erstes Thema.      (G-Dur.)              (Bearbeitung der             (G-Dur.)
   (G-Dur.)   .  .  .  .  .  .  .  .  .  .   beiden Themas.)  .  .  .  .  .  .  .  .  .  .  .  .          Zweites.
                                                                                                        (G-Dur.)
```

7. Rudolph Steglich, *Robert Schummans Kinderszenen* (Kassel und Basel: Bärenreiter-Verlag, 1949).

18. Robert Schumann, *Gesammelte Schriften über Musik und Musiker* (Leipzig: Breitkopf und Härtel, 1914), Vol. I, p. 70.

19. Robert Schumann, quoted in Hans Joachim Moser & Eberhard Rebling, *Robert Schumann* (Leipzig: Breitkopf und Härtel, 1956), p. 131.

20. Robert Schumann, *Gesammelte Schriften über Musik und Musiker* (Leipzig: Breitkopf und Härtel, 1914), Vol. I, p. 498.

221. *Ibid.*, Vol. II, p. 94.

22. Robert Schumann, *Robert Schumanns Briefe*, edited by F. Gustav Jansen (Leipzig: Breitkopf und Härtel, 1904), p. 322.

23. See *supra*, Chapter II, p. 19.

24. Carl Maria von Weber, quoted in Paul Moos, *Die Philosophie der Musik* (Berlin: Schuster und Loeffler, 1922), p. 187.

25. Robert Schumann, quoted in Hans Joachim Moser & Eberhard Rebling, *Robert Schumann* (Leipzig: Breitkopf und Härtel, 1956), p. 109.

26. Robert Schumann, *Gesammelte Schriften über Musik und Musiker* (Leipzig: Breitkopf und Härtel, 1914), Vol. I, p. 84.

27. Robert Schumann, quoted in Dagmar Weise, "Ein bisher verschollenes Manuskript zu Schumanns Album für die Jugend", *Festschrift für Joseph Schmidt-Görg* (Bonn, 1957), 388.

228. Robert Schumann, *Gesammelte Schriften über Musik und Musiker* (Leipzig: Breitkopf und Härtel, 1914), Vol. I, p. 137.

229. Rudolph Steglich, "Zwei Titelzeichnungen zu Robert Schumanns Jugendalbum als Interpretations-dokument", *Deutsches Jahrbuch der Musikwissenschaft* (1960), 38.

230. Robert Schumann, *Gesammelte Schriften über Musik und Musiker* (Leipzig: Breitkopf und Härtel, 1914), Vol. I, p. 435.

231. *Ibid.*, p. 85.

232. *Ibid.*, p. 368.

233. *Ibid.*, p. 84.

234. Robert Schumann, quoted in Wolfgang Boetticher, *Robert Schumann: Einführung in Persönlichkeit und Werk* (Berlin: Hahnefeld, 1941), pp. 205-206.

235. See *supra*, Chapter II, p. 15.

236. Robert Schumann, quoted in Karl Heinrich Wörner, *Robert Schumann* (Zürich: Atlantis, 1949), p. 31.

237. Robert Schumann, quoted and translated in Robert L. Jacobs, "Schumann and Jean Paul", *Music and Letters*, XXX (1949), 251.

238. Robert Schumann, *Jugendbriefe* (Leipzig: Breitkopf und Härtel, 1886), p. 17.

239. Robert Schumann, quoted in Wolfgang Boetticher, *Robert Schumann in seinen Schriften und Briefen* (Berlin: Hahnefeld, 1942), p. 168.

240. Robert Schumann, quoted in Karl Heinrich Wörner, *Robert Schumann* (Zürich: Atlantis, 1949), p. 64.

196

241. René Wellek, *A History of Modern Criticism, 1750-1950* (New Haven: Yale University Press, 1955), Vol. II, p. 102. Schumann encounters the idea of *Doppelnatur* not only in Jean Paul but also in the works of E. T. A. Hoffmann, and more specifically in the character of Kapellmeister Kreisler. It is, therefore, not surprising to find Schumann basing a series of piano pieces, *Kreisleriana*, on episodes from the life of this fictitious personality.

242. Robert Schumann, quoted in Karl Heinrich Wörner, *Robert Schumann* (Zürich: Atlantis, 1949), p. 9.

243. Robert Schumann, quoted in F. Gustav Jansen, *Die Davidsbündler* (Leipzig: Breitkopf und Härtel, 1883), p. 26.

244. *Ibid.*, p. 19.

245. Robert Schumann, quoted and translated in Gerald Abraham, *Schumann: A Symposium* (London: Oxford University Press, 1952), p. 8.

246. Robert Schumann, quoted in Wolfgang Boetticher, *Robert Schumann: Einführung in Persönlichkeit und Werk* (Berlin: Hahnefeld, 1941), p. 320.

247. Robert Schumann, quoted in Wolfgang Boetticher, *Robert Schumann: Einführung in Persönlichkeit und Werk* (Berlin: Hahnefeld, 1941), p. 317.

248. Robert Schumann, *Gesammelte Schriften über Musik und Musiker* (Leipzig: Breitkopf und Härtel, 1914), Vol. I, pp. 84-85.

249. *Ibid.*, p. 65.

250. Robert Schumann, quoted in Wolfgang Boetticher, *Robert Schumann: Einführung in Persönlichkeit und Werk* (Berlin: Hahnefeld, 1941), p. 220.

251. Marcel Brion, *Schumann and The Romantic Age*, translated by Geoffrey Sainsbury (New York: The Macmillan Company, 1956), p. 134.

252. Robert Schumann, quoted in A. Steiner, "Robert Schumann", *99. Neujahrsblatt der allgemeinen Musikgesellschaft in Zürich auf das Jahr 1911*, p. 6.

253. Robert Schumann, *Robert Schumanns Briefe*, edited by F. Gustav Jansen (Leipzig: Breitkopf und Härtel, 1904), p. 43.

254. Robert Schumann, *Jugendbriefe* (Leipzig: Breitkopf und Härtel, 1886), pp. 166-167.

255. *Ibid.*, pp. 167-168.

256. Robert Schumann, quoted in Hermann Erler, *Robert Schumanns Leben und Werke aus seinen Briefen geschildert* (Leipzig: Ries & Erler, 1887), Vol. I, pp. 50-51.

257. Jean Paul, quoted and translated in Gerald Abraham, *Schumann: A Symposium* (London: Oxford University Press, 1952), p. 38.

258. Robert Schumann, quoted and translated in Gerald Abraham, *Schumann: A Symposium* (London: Oxford University Press, 1952), p. 10.

259. Jean Paul, quoted and translated in Gerald Abraham, *Schu-*

mann: A Symposium (London: Oxford University Press, 1952), p. 39.

260. Robert Schumann, *Robert Schumanns Briefe*, edited by F. Gustav Jansen (Leipzig: Breitkopf und Härtel, 1904), pp. 101-102.

261. Robert Schumann, quoted in J. Gensel, "Robert Schumanns Briefwechsel mit Henriette Voigt," *Die Grenzboten* (Leipzig: Grunow, 1892), p. 325.

262. Robert Schumann, *Gesammelte Schriften über Musik und Musiker* (Leipzig: Breitkopf und Härtel, 1914), Vol. I, p. 484.

263. Marcel Brion, *Schumann and The Romantic Age*, translated by Geoffrey Sainsbury (New York: The Macmillan Company, 1956), p. 46.

264. Robert Schumann, *Robert Schumanns Briefe*, edited by F. Gustav Jansen (Leipzig: Breitkopf und Härtel, 1904), p. 170.

265. Robert Schumann, quoted in Wolfgang Boetticher, *Robert Schumann: Einführung in Persönlichkeit und Werk* (Berlin: Hahnefeld, 1941), p. 208.

266. Robert Schumann, quoted in Rudolph Steglich, *Robert Schumanns Kinderszenen* (Kassel und Basel: Bärenreiter-Verlag, 1949), p. 5.

267. Marcel Brion, *Schumann and The Romantic Age*, translated by Geoffrey Sainsbury (New York: The Macmillan Company, 1956), p. 194.

268. Robert Schumann, *Robert Schumanns Briefe*, edited by F. Gustav Jansen (Leipzig: Breitkopf und Härtel, 1904), p. 148.

269. Robert Schumann, quoted in Berthold Litzmann, *Clara Schumann: Ein Künstlerleben* (Leipzig: Breitkopf und Härtel, 1905-1909), Vol. I, p. 206.

270. Robert Schumann, quoted in Paula & Walter Rehberg, *Robert Schumann* (Zürich & Stuttgart: Artemis, 1954), p. 457.

271. Jacques Barzun, *Berlioz and the Romantic Century* (Boston: Little, Brown & Co., 1950), pp. 372-373.

BIBLIOGRAPHY

PRIMARY SOURCES

Altmann, Wilhelm. "Bisher unveröffentliche Briefe Robert Schumanns," *Die Musik*, Jg. XV (1922-23).

Altmann, Wilhelm. "Vier Briefe Richard Wagners an Robert Schumann," *Die Musik*, Jg. IV (1904-05).

Becker, Martha. "Neue Briefe von Robert Schumann an Karl Kossmaly," *Die Musik* (January, 1942).

Beethoven, Ludwig van. *The Nine Symphonies of Beethoven in Score*. Edited and devised by Albert E. Wier. New York: Harcourt, Brace and Company, 1935.

Beethoven, Ludwig van. *Five Piano Concertos*. Kalmus Miniature Orchestra Scores. New York: Kalmus, n.d.

Beethoven, Ludwig van. *The Letters of Beethoven*. Edited and translated by Emily Anderson. New York: St. Martin's Press, 1961.

Beethoven, Ludwig van. *Sonatas For Pianoforte and Violin*. New York: Carl Fischer, 1917.

Boetticher, Wolfgang. *Robert Schumann in seinen Schriften und Briefen*. Berlin: B. Hahnefeld, 1942.

Brendel, Franz. "Robert Schumann mit Rücksicht auf Mendelssohn-Bartholdy und die Entwicklung der modernen Tonkunst überhaupt," *Neue Zeitschrift für Musik*, No. 15 (February 19, 1845).

Callomon, Fritz T. "Unbekannte Briefe Robert und Clara Schumann," *Neue Zeitschrift für Musik* (1956).

Eismann, Georg. *Robert Schumann*. Leipzig: Breitkopf und Härtel, 1956. 2 vols.

Erler, Hermann. "Ein ungedruckter Canon und sechs ungedruckte Haus-und Lebensregeln Robert Schumann," *Die Musik*, Jg. V (1905-06).

Erler, Hermann. *Robert Schumanns Leben und Werke aus seinen Briefen geschildert*. Leipzig: Ries & Erler, 1887.

Erler, Hermann. "Zwei ungedruckte Briefe von Robert Schumann," *Die Musik*, Jg. II (1903).

Flechsig, Emil. "Erinnerungen an Robert Schumann," *Neue Zeitschrift für Musik* (1956).

Gensel, J. "Robert Schumanns Briefwechsel mit Henriette Voigt," *Die Grenzboten*. Leipzig: Grunow (1892).

Hollander, Hans. "Ein Brief Robert Schumanns an den schwedischen Musiker L. Norman," *Neue Zeitschrift für Musik* (1960).

Jansen, F. Gustav. "Briefwechsel zwischen Robert Franz und Robert Schumann," *Die Musik*, Jg. VIII (1908-09).

Jansen, F. Gustav. "Ein unbekannter Brief von Robert Schumann," *Die Musik*, Jg. V (1905-06).

Liszt, Franz. *Six Grand Études after Paganini*. Critically revised by Paolo Gallico. New York: Schirmer, 1906, 1934.

Litzmann, Berthold. *Clara Schumann: Ein Künstlerleben*. Leipzig: Breitkopf und Härtel, 1905-09, Vol. I.

Montaigne, Michel de. *The Essays*. Translated by John Florio. New York & London: The Knickerbocker Press, 1907.

Paganini, Nicolo. *24 Capricen für Violin Solo*. Opus 1. Edited by Carl Flesch. Leipzig: Peters, n.d.

Pohl, R. "Erinnerungen an Robert Schumann," *Deutsche Revue*, Vol. II (August and September, 1878).

Richter, Johann Paul Friedrich. *Flegeljahre*. Weimar: Hermann Böhlau, 1934.

Richter, Johann Paul Friedrich. *Vorschule der Ästhetik*. Weimar: Hermann Böhlau, 1935.

Schnapp, Friedrich. "Eine unbekannte Rezension Robert Schumanns," *Neue Zeitschrift für Musik* (1925).

Schnapp, Friedrich. "Essai de reconstitution de la correspondence de Schumann et de Liszt," *La Revue Musicale* (1935).

Schumann, Alfred. *Der Junge Schumann: Dichtungen und Briefe*. Leipzig: Insel-Verlag, 1910.

Schumann, Eugenie. *Robert Schumann: Ein Lebensbild meines Vaters*. Leipzig: Koehler & Amelang, 1931.

Schumann, Eugenie. *Erinnerungen*. Stuttgart: J. Engelhorns, 1927.

Schumann, Ferdinand. "Ein unbekannter Jugendbrief von Robert Schumann," *Die Musik*, Jg. IX (1909-10).

Schumann, Robert. *Complete Works for Piano Solo*. Edited by Clara Schumann. New York: Kalmus, n.d. 6 vols.

Schumann, Robert. *Erinnerungen an Felix Mendelssohn-Bartholdy*. Zwickau: Predella-Verlag, 1947.

Schumann, Robert. *Gesammelte Schriften über Musik und Musiker*. Leipzig: G. Wigand, 1854. 4 vols. in 2.

Schumann, Robert. *Gesammelte Schriften über Musik und Musiker*. Leipzig: Breitkopf und Härtel, 1914.

Schumann, Robert. *Gesammelte Schriften über Musik und Musiker*. Edited by Paul Bekker. Berlin: Wegweiser-Verlag, 1922.

Schumann, Robert. *Jugendbriefe*. Leipzig: Breitkopf und Härtel, 1886.

Schumann, Robert. *Robert Schumanns Briefe*. Edited by F. Gustav Jansen. Leipzig: Breitkopf und Härtel, 1904.

Schumann, Robert. "Wie kann man aus den Spielen, die jemand liebt, auf seinen Charakter schliessen?" *Neue Zeitschrift für Musik* (1959).

Thibaut, Anton Friedrich. *Ueber Reinheit der Tonkunst*. Heidelberg: Mohr, 1875.

Wasielewski, Wilhelm Joseph von. *Life of Robert Schumann*. Translated by A. L. Alger. Boston: Oliver Ditson, 1871.

Wasielewski, Wilhelm Joseph von. *Schumanniana*. Bonn: Emil Strauss, 1883.

Weise, Dagmar. "Ein bisher verschollenes Manuskript zu Schumanns Album für die Jugend," *Festschrift für Joseph Schmidt-Görg*. Bonn: Beethovenhaus, 1957.

SECONDARY SOURCES

Abert, Hermann Joseph. *Robert Schumann.* Berlin: Schlesische Verlagsanstalt, 1909.

Abraham, Gerald. "Recent Research on Schumann," *Proceedings of the Royal Music Association* (1948-49).

Abraham, Gerald. "Schumann's Opus II and III," *Monthly Musical Record,* Vol. LXXVI (1946).

Abraham, Gerald. *Schumann: A Symposium.* London: Oxford University Press, 1952.

d'Albert, Marguerite. *Robert Schumann: son oeuvre de piano.* Paris: Fischbasher, 1904.

Alf, Julius. "Der Kritiker Robert Schumann," *Nieder Rheinische Musikfest* (1956).

Ambros, A. W. "Robert Schumanns Tage und Werke," *Culturhistorische Bilder aus der Gegenwart.* Leipzig: H. Matthes, 1860.

Barzun, Jacques. *Berlioz and the Romantic Century.* Boston: Little, Brown and Company, 1950.

Basch, Victor. *La vie douloureuse de Schumann.* Paris: F. Alcan, 1928.

Basch, Victor. "L'esthétique de Schumann," *La Revue Musicale* (1935).

Basch, Victor. *Schumann.* Paris: F. Alcan, 1926.

Baser, Friedrich. "Ein Student in Heidelberg," *Musica,* Jg. X (1956).

Beaufils, Marcel. *La Musique de Piano de Schumann.* Paris: Librarie Larousse, 1951.

Berg, Alban. "Die Musikalische Impotenz der 'Neuen Ästhetik Hans Pfitzners'," *Musikblätter des Anbruch,* Jg. II, Nos. 11-12 (1920).

Boetticher, Wolfgang. "Ein Neuer Marsch von Robert Schumann," *Die Musik,* Jg. XXXIII (1941).

Boetticher, Wolfgang. *Robert Schumann: Einführung in Persönlichkeit und Werk.* Berlin: B. Hahnefeld, 1941.

Boetticher, Wolfgang. "Robert Schumann in seinen Beziehungen zu Johannes Brahms," *Die Musik,* Jg. XXIX (1937).

Bouyer, R. "Schumann et la musique a programme," *Le Ménéstrel* (1903).

Brion, Marcel. *Schumann and The Romantic Age.* New York: The Macmillan Company, 1956.

Bücken, Ernst. *Robert Schumann.* Cologne: Staufen-Verlag, 1940.

Bugard, Pierre. "L'Ame de Schumann," *La Revue Musicale* (1935).

Burckhardt, Jacob. *The Civilization of the Renaissance in Italy.* Translated by G. C. Middlemore. London: George G. Harrap & Company, 1929.

Calvocoressi, Michel D. *Schumann.* Paris: Société des éditions Louis-Michaud, 1912.

Carner, Mosco. *Studien zur Sonatenform bei Robert Schumann.* Wiener Diss., 1928.

Chalupt, René. "Schumann musicien poète," *La Revue Musicale* (1935).

Chantavoine, Jean. "La jeunesse de Schumann," *Musiciens et poètes.* Paris: F. Alcan, 1912.

Chévilliard, Camille. "Schumann," *Le Courier Musical* (1906).
Chissell, Joan. *Schumann.* London: J. M. Dent, 1948.
Colling, Alfred. *La Vie de Robert Schumann.* Paris: Gallimard, 1931.
Dadelsen, Georg von. *Altersstil und alte Techniken in der Musik des 19. Jahrhunderts.* Berliner Diss., 1951.
Dadelsen, Georg von. "Robert Schumann und die Musik Bachs," *Archiv für Musikwissenschaft,* Jg. XIV (1957).
Dahms, Walter. *Schumann.* Berlin: Schuster und Loeffler, 1916.
Dieters, Hermann. "Besprechung: Robert Schumann, Gesammelte Schriften über Musik und Musiker," *Vierteljahrsschrift für Musikwissenschaft,* IX (1893).
Dieters, Hermann. "Robert Schumann als Schriftsteller," *Allgemeine Musikalische Zeitung,* Numbers 47, 48, 49 (November 22, 1865).
Duval, R. "L'Amour du poète de Schumann-Heine," *Rivista Musicale Italiana,* Vol. VIII (1901).
Einstein, Alfred. *Die Romantik in der Musik.* Wien: Bergland-Verlag, 1950.
Einstein, Alfred. "Opus 1," *Von Schütz bis Hindemith.* Zürich: Pan-Verlag, 1957.
Eismann, Georg. *Erinnerungen an Mendelssohn-Bartholdy.* Zwickau: Sachsen Predella-Verlag, 1948.
Eismann, Georg. *Robert Schumann, eine Biographie in Wort und Bild.* Leipzig: Breitkopf und Härtel, 1956.
Eismann, Georg. "Robert Schumann als Pianist," *Neue Zeitschrift für Musik,* 1951.
Elliot, J. H. *Berlioz.* London: J. M. Dent & Sons, Ltd., 1938.
Ferguson, Donald M. *A History of Musical Thought.* New York and London: Appleton-Century-Crofts, Inc., 1948.
Flinsch, Erich. "Ludwig Schunke," *Neue Zeitschrift für Musik* (1960).
Forger, Inge. "Schöpferische Musikkritik," *Neue Zeitschrift für Musik* (1956).
Frömbgen-Essen, Hanns. "Hegel und die musikalische Romantik-Die Erhellung der Musik durch die Philosophie," *Die Musik,* Jg. XXI (1929).
Fuller-Maitland, J. A. *Schumann's Pianoforte Works.* London: Oxford University Press, 1927.
Gatz, Felix. *Musik-Ästhetik in ihren Hauptrichtungen.* Stuttgart: F. Enke, 1929.
Geiger, Benno. "Phantasiestück von Schumann: eine Deutung," *Zeitschrift für Musik,* Vol. XCVIII (1902).
Geiringer, Karl. "Ein unbekanntes Klavierwerk aus Schumanns Jugendzeit," *Die Musik,* Jg. XXV (1933).
Geiringer, Karl. "Schumann in Wien," *Zeitschrift für Musik* (1931).
Georgii, Walter. *Klaviermusik.* Zürich: Atlantis, 1950.
Gertler, Wolfgang. *Robert Schumann in seinen frühen Klavierwerken.* Leipzig: Druck von Radelli & Hille, 1931.
Glöckner, Ernst. *Studien zur romantischen Psychologie der Musik.* München: G. C. Steinicke, 1909.

Goldenberg, Rosalie. *Der Klaviersatz bei Schumann*. Wiener Diss., 1931.

Gurlitt, Willibald. "Robert Schumann in seinen Skizzen gegenüber Beethoven," *Kongressbericht der Beethoven-Zentenarfeier*. Wien: March, 1927.

Hadow, W. H. "Robert Schumann and the Romantic Movement in Germany," *Studies in Modern Music*. 4th ed. London: Seeley and Company, 1898.

Hase, Oskar, V. "Robert Schumann," *Gedenkschrift*, Vol. II. Leipzig: Breitkopf und Härtel, 1919.

Hegel, Georg. *Science of Logic*. Translated by W. H. Johnston and L. G. Struthers. New York: Macmillan, 1929.

Hernried, Robert. "Four Unpublished Compositions by Robert Schumann," *Musical Quarterly*, Vol. XXVIII (1942).

Hirschberg, Leopold. "Merkwürdiges aus einem Schumann-Erstdruck," *Die Musik*, Jg. XXI (1929).

Hohenemser, Richard. "Formale Eigentümlichkeiten in Robert Schumanns Klaviermusik," *Festschrift zum 50. Geburtstag von Adolf Sandberger*. München: F. Zierfuss, 1918.

Hohenemser, Richard. "Robert Schumann unter dem Einfluss der Alten," *Die Musik*, Jg. IX (1909-10).

Holroyd, Charles. *Michael Angelo Buonarroti*. London: Duckworth and Company, 1903.

Huber, Kurt. *Musikästhetik*. Stuttgart: Ettal, Buch-Kunst-Verlag, 1954.

Huschke, Konrad. *Robert Schumanns Beziehungen zu Felix-Mendelssohn-Bartholdy, Richard Wagner und Franz Liszt*. Pritzwalk: A. Tienken, 1928.

Jacobs, Robert L. "Schumann and Jean Paul," *Music and Letters*, Vol. XXX (1949).

Jansen, F. Gustav. "Aus Robert Schumanns Schulzeit," *Die Musik*, Jg. V, No. 20 (1905-06).

Jansen, F. Gustav. *Die Davidsbündler*. Leipzig: Breitkopf und Härtel, 1883.

Jansen, F. Gustav. "Schumann und Vesque von Pütlingen," *Die Grenzboten* (1894).

Jonas, A. "Das Skizzenbuch zu Schumanns Jugendalbum," *Zeitschrift für Musik* (1931).

Kapp, Julius. "Schumanns Études Symphoniques, Opus 13," *Die Musik*, Jg. IX (1909-10).

Knayer, C. "Robert Schumann als Meister der rhythmischen Verschiebungen," *Musikpädagogische Blätter*, Jg. XXXVII, No. 9 (May 1, 1914).

Knayer, C. "Schumanns Klavierstil," *Neue Musikzeitung*, No. 24 (1911).

Koechlin, Charles. "Schumann, Musicien romantique, national et universel," *La Revue Musicale* (1935).

Kötz, Hans. *Der Einfluss Jean Pauls auf Robert Schumann.* Weimar: H. Böhlau Nachfolger, 1933.

Komerzynski, Egon V. "Schumann und die Romantik," *Neue Musikzeitung* (1906).

Korte, Werner. *Robert Schumann.* Potsdam: Akademische Verlagsgesellschaft Athenaion, m.b.H., 1937.

Kretschmar, Hermann. "Robert Schumann als Ästhetiker," *Peters-Jahrbuch*, 13 (1906).

Kretschmar, Hermann. "I. Kant, Musikauffassung und ihr Einfluss auf die folgende Zeit," *Peters-Jahrbuch* (1904).

deLeeuwe, Hans. "Zur Deutung der 'Kinderszenen'," *Neue Zeitschrift für Musik* (1956).

Leipold, Eugen. "Von Melodieklang in Schumanns Klaviermusik," *Neue Zeitschrift für Musik* (1956).

Lichtenberger, Henri. "Schumann et le temps présent," *La Revue Musicale* (1935).

Lippmann, Edward A. "Robert Schumann," *Die Musik in Geschichte und Gegenwart*, Vol. XII, 271-326.

Lippmann, Edward A. "Theory and Practice in Schumann's Aesthetics," *Journal of the American Musicological Society*, 1964.

Lübke, G. von. "Schumann und die Programmusik," *Neue Musikzeitung* (1906).

Mäcklenburg, Albert. "Liszt in seinen Beziehungen zu Robert Schumann," *Der Klavierlehrer*, Jg. XXVIII, Nos. 8, 9, 11, 12 (1905).

Mäcklenburg, Albert. "Robert Schumann's Erstlingswerke," *Musikpädagogische Blätter*, No. 4 (1916).

Mauclair, Camille. "La Musique de Piano de Schumann," *Le Courier Musical* (1906).

Mauclair, Camille. *Schumann.* Paris: H. Laurens, 1906.

Minotti, Giovanni. "Die Enträtselung des Schumann'schen Abegg-Geheimnisses," *Zeitschrift für Musik* (1927).

Minotti, Giovanni. *Die Enträtselung des Schumann'schen Sphinx-Geheimnisses.* Leipzig: L. Doblinger, 1924.

Minotti, Giovanni. "Schumann: Fantasie in C Dur," *Die Geheimdokumente der Davidsbündler.* Leipzig: Steingräber Verlag, 1934.

Moos, Paul. *Die Philosophie der Musik.* Berlin: Schuster und Loeffler, 1922.

Moos, Paul. *Moderne Musikästhetik in Deutschland.* Leipzig: H. Seemann Nachfolger, 1902.

Moser, Hans Joachim & Eberhard Rebling. *Robert Schumann.* Leipzig: Breitkopf und Härtel, 1956.

Müller, Ernst. *Robert Schumann, eine Bildnisstudie.* Olten: Otto Walter, 1950.

Músiol, Robert. "Der Takt bei Robert Schumann," *Neue Zeitschrift für Musik* (1901).

Nagel, Willibald. "Schumann und Wir," *Neue Zeitschrift für Musik* (1906).

Nef, Karl. "Eine Kritik Robert Schumanns als ein Musiker," *Aufsätze.* Basel: Baseler Berichthaus, 1936.

Niecks, Frederick. *Robert Schumann*. London: J. M. Dent & Sons, Ltd., 1925.

Niemann, Walter. "Zum 50. Todestage Robert Schumanns," *Neue Zeitschrift für Musik* (1906).

Ninck, Martin Hermann. *Schumann und die Romantik in der Musik*. Heidelberg: Niels Kampmann, 1929.

Noren-Herzberg, O. "Robert Schumann als Musikschriftsteller," *Die Musik*, Jg. V (1905-06).

Parrott, Ian. "A Plea for Schumann's Opus 11," *Music and Letters*. Vol. XXXIII, No. 1 (1952).

Pessenlehner, R. "Robert Schumann und die Neue Zeitschrift für Musik," *Neue Zeitschrift für Musik*. Jg. C (1933).

Petzoldt, Richard. *Robert Schuman, sein Leben in Bildern*. Leipzig: Bibliographisches Institut, 1956.

Petzoldt, Richard. *Robert Schumann, Leben und Werk*. Leipzig: Breitkopf und Härtel, 1941.

Pfordten, Hermann Ludwig, Freiherr von der. *Robert Schumann*. Leipzig: Quelle und Meyer, 1920.

Pfrogner, Hermann. *Musik, Geschichte ihrer Deutung*. Freiburg: K. Alber, 1954.

Pitrou, Robert. "D'Eusebius à Florestan," *La Revue Musicale* (1935).

Pitrou, Robert. *La vie intérieure de R. Schumann*. Paris: H. Laurens, 1925.

Puttmann, Max. "Robert Schumann in seinen Klavierwerken," *Musik Wochenblatt*, vereinigt mit N.Z.f.M. Leipzig: Jg. XLI, No. 9/10 (1910).

Redenbacher, Else. "Schumann als Erzieher," *Musik Wochenblatt*, vereinigt mit N.Z.f.M. Leipzig: Jg. XLI, No. 9/10 (1910).

Redlich, H. F. "Schumann Discoveries," *Monthly Musical Record*. Vol. LXXX (1950).

Rehberg, Paula & Walter. *Robert Schumann*. Zürich and Stuttgart: Artemis, 1954.

Reissmann, August. *Robert Schumann, sein Leben und seine Werke*. Berlin: J. Guttentag, 1879.

Schäfke, Rudolph. *Geschichte der Musikästhetik in Umrissen*. Berlin: M. Hesse, 1934.

Schenk, Erich. "Robert Schumann und Peter Lindpainter in Wien," *Festschrift Joseph Schmidt-Görg zum 60. Geburtstag*. Bonn: Beethovenhaus, 1957.

Schering, Arnold. "Robert Schumann als Tragiker," *Neue Zeitschrift für Musik* (1901).

Schering, Arnold. "Träumerei," *Musikalische Bildung*. Leipzig: Quelle und Meyer, 1911.

Schmidt, Leopold. "Robert Schumann," *Die Musik*. Jg. V (1905-06).

Schmitz, Arnold. "Anfänge der Ästhetik R. Schumanns," *Zeitschrift für Musikwissenschaft*, Jg. II, No. 9 (June, 1920).

Schmitz, Arnold. "Die ästhetischen Anschauungen Robert Schumanns in ihren Beziehungen zur Romantischen Literatur," *Zeitschrift für Musikwissenschaft*, Jg. III (1920/1921).

Schmitz, Arnold. "Wie steht Schumann theoretisch zur Programmmusik?" *Neue Musikzeitung*. Jg. XLII, No. 9 (1921).

Schmitz, Eugen. "Denkwürdige Musikbeilagen zu Robert Schumanns Zeitschrift," *Deutsche Musikkultur* (1941).

Schnapp, Friedrich. *Heinrich Heine und Robert Schumann*. Hamburg, Berlin: Hoffmann und Campe, 1924.

Schneider, Louis and Marcel Mareschal. *Schumann sa vie et ses oeuvres*. Paris: E. Fasquelle, 1905.

Schulze, Herbert. *Zur Frage der ästhetischen Anschauungen Robert Schumanns*. Dresden: MS, 1954.

Schumann, Eugenie. "The Diary of Robert and Clara Schumann," *Music and Letters*. Vol. XV, 1934.

Schwarz, Werner. *Robert Schumann und die Variation*. Kassel: Bärenreiter-Verlag, 1932.

Schweiger, M. *Die Harmonik in den Klavierwerken Schumanns*. Wiener Diss., 1931.

Seidl, Arthur. "Robert Schumann und die Neudeutschen," *Wagneriana*, Vol. II. Berlin & Leipzig: Schuster und Loeffler, 1901.

Serauky, Walter. *Die Musikalische Nachahmungsästhetik*. Münster: Helios-Verlag, 1929.

Siegmund-Schultze, Walther. "Wort und Ton bei Robert Schumann," *Kongress-Bericht Gesellschaft für Musikforschung*. Kassel und Basel: Bärenreiter-Verlag, 1956.

Simon, James. "Robert Schumanns Klaviermusik," *Allgemeine Musikzeitung* (1910).

Spitta, Philipp. *Ein Lebensbild Robert Schumanns*. Leipzig: Breitkopf und Härtel, 1882.

Spitta, Philipp. "Über Robert Schumanns Schriften," *Musikgeschichtliche Aufsätze*. Berlin: Paetel, 1894.

Stam, Henk. "Schumanns Rückschau auf Bach," *Neue Zeitschrift für Musik* (1956).

Steglich, Rudolph. *Robert Schumanns Kinderszenen*. Kassel und Basel: Bärenreiter-Verlag, 1949.

Steglich, Rudolph. "Zwei Titelzeichnungen zu Robert Schumanns Jugendalbum als Interpretationsdokumente," *Deutsches Jahrbuch der Musikwissenschaft* (1960).

Stein, Fritz. "Schumann als Student in Heidelberg," *Neue Musikzeitung* (1906).

Steiner, A. "Robert Schumann," *99. Neujahrsblatt der allgemeinen Musikgesellschaft in Zürich auf das Jahr 1911*.

Sternfeld, Richard. "Einige Bemerkungen zum Schaffen Robert Schumanns," *Die Musik*, Jg. IX (1909-10).

Stieglitz, Olga. *Einführung in die Musikästhetik*. Stuttgart and Berlin: Cottascher-Verlag, 1928.

Straeten, E. van der. "Mendelssohns und Schumanns Beziehungen zu J. H. Lübeck und J. J. H. Verhulst," *Die Musik*, Jg. III (1903-04).

Straeten, E. van der. "Streiflichter auf Mendelssohns und Schumanns Beziehungen zu zeitgenössischen Musikern," *Die Musik*, Jg. IV (1904-05).

Sullivan, J. W. N. *Beethoven: His Spiritual Development.* New York: Alfred Knopf, 1927.

Sutermeister, Peter. *Robert Schumann.* Zürich: Ex-libris-Verlag, 1949.

Tessmer, Hans. *Robert Schumann.* Stuttgart: J. Engelhorn, 1930.

Tiersot, Julien. "Schumann et Berlioz," *La Revue Musicale* (1935).

Valentin, Erich. "Der andere Schumann," *Neue Zeitschrift für Musik* (1956).

Valentin, Erich. "Robert Schumann, Werk und Vermächtnis," *Neue Zeitschrift für Musik* (1940).

Wagner, Kurt. *Robert Schumann als Schüler und Abiturient.* Zwickau: i.S., Geschäftsstelle der Robert-Schumanngesellschaft Nr. 2, 1928.

Wellek, René. *A History of Modern Criticism, 1750-1950.* New Haven: Yale University Press, 1955. 2 vols.

Wörner, Karl Heinrich. *Robert Schumann.* Zürich: Atlantis, 1949.

Wolff, Helmut Christian. "Robert Schumann—der Klassizist," *Musica* (1948).

Wustmann, Gustav. "Zur Entstehungsgeschichte der Schumannischen Zeitschrift für Musik," *Zeitschrift der Internationalen Musikgesellschaft*, Jg. VIII (1907).

Young, Percy M. *Tragic Muse, The Life and Works of Robert Schumann.* London: Dobson, 1961.